To

Lonny

With all our love

Mom & Dad

BLIND COURAGE

A 2,000-Mile Journey of Faith

To my children — Marianne, Billy, and Jeff:

Family, forgivers, and friends

First published in the United States of America in 1992 by WRS Publishing,
A Division of WRS Group, Inc., 701 N. New Road, Waco, TX 76710
Design by Jean Norwood and Linda Filgo

10 9 8 7 6 5 4 3 2

The Seeing Eye is a registered trademark.
M&M'S Chocolate Candies are made by M&M-Mars.
Valium is a registered trademark of Roche Products Inc.
Milkbones is a registered trademark of Nabisco Foods Co.

Library of Congress Catalog Card Number 92-60012
Irwin, Bill
McCasland, David
Blind Courage

ISBN 0-941539-86-5

BLIND COURAGE

A 2,000-Mile Journey of Faith

To my children — Marianne, Billy, and Jeff:

Family, forgivers, and friends

First published in the United States of America in 1992 by WRS Publishing, A Division of WRS Group, Inc., 701 N. New Road, Waco, TX 76710
Design by Jean Norwood and Linda Filgo

10 9 8 7 6 5 4 3 2

The Seeing Eye is a registered trademark.
M&M'S Chocolate Candies are made by M&M-Mars.
Valium is a registered trademark of Roche Products Inc.
Milkbones is a registered trademark of Nabisco Foods Co.

Library of Congress Catalog Card Number 92-60012
Irwin, Bill
McCasland, David
Blind Courage

ISBN 0-941539-86-5

BLIND COURAGE

By Bill Irwin
with David McCasland

WRS
PUBLISHING

A Division of WRS Group, Inc.
Waco, Texas

Contents

Foreword by
Dr. Robert Schuller

Bill Irwin and his book will teach you, they will motivate you, and they will inspire you. There is no doubt that this man is a living miracle. Although he is blind, Bill, with his Seeing Eye dog, Orient, walked the entire Appalachian Trail—2,168 miles in snow, rain, and summer heat.

But there are more miracles! Bill broke a rib, had many falls, ran into a live bear, and managed to survive some other close calls along the way... this is truly one of the most amazing stories I have ever read. While reading Bill's story, decide for yourself. Does Christianity really make a difference? Does a positive faith permanently change lives on the deepest level?

When I met Bill in the Crystal Cathedral as my guest on *Hour of Power*, I was reminded of how vividly one's face reflects the honesty of the heart. Bill has beautiful eyes and a beautiful face. The subconscious is a hint of the conscious. Looking at Bill, I could see into the subconscious of the man standing before me. It is the spirit, the very familiar spirit that lives in me too. So I felt very close to Bill Irwin, even though I had never met him before. Because that same spirit is the spirit of Jesus Christ. Somehow he came into the life of Bill Irwin and saved him.

God loves Bill Irwin and so do I. You will love him, and you'll also feel closer to the spirit of Jesus Christ, when you read this inspirational story, *Blind Courage*. I have been so blessed by Bill's book. May you also be blessed.

Dr. Robert H. Schuller

Preface

Before you read this book, try a simple experiment. Walk across a familiar room with your eyes closed. Even though you know the room, obstacles will present themselves. Now, imagine hiking more than two thousand miles over unfamiliar terrain with your eyes closed, and you'll have some idea of how challenging it was for Bill Irwin to hike the Appalachian Trail.

My first encounter with Bill and his Seeing Eye dog, Orient, was on the Trail. My son, David, and I had just a short time to spare during a trip to Washington, D.C., and decided to check out the newspaper story of a blind man who was thru-hiking the A.T.

Knowing only that Bill was within twenty miles of where a highway crossed the A.T. near Washington, we parked our rental car and decided to take an hour's walk along the Trail in one direction. If we didn't run into Bill and Orient, we would just forget the matter.

Within the first two hundred yards of our walk, we came upon Bill and Orient. In the next few hours, I realized this man was for real. Weeks later, we convinced Bill that his story should be published. This book is the result.

Once you read Bill's story, you will never forget him.

Bill was an angry, middle-aged man with few prospects and fewer friends. His four marriages had failed. He was an alcoholic, a five-pack-a-day smoker, a manipulator, a user, and a rare eye disease had left him blind and embittered.

But the Bill Irwin who sat alone night after night drinking himself into oblivion, who refused to get a Seeing Eye dog because it might inhibit his amorous pursuits, became a hero. He is now a much-in-demand speaker and a symbol of hope and pride for millions of physically challenged Americans.

For Bill Irwin walked the entire length of the Appalachian Trail. He walked it on faith and sheer determination, starting in the chilly March rains of the mountains of Georgia, and finishing in November blizzards in the mountains of Maine.

Along the way he survived several hair-breadth brushes with death, a curious bear, and a horde of field mice. He endured broken ribs and enough falls to last several lifetimes. He encountered an array of inspirational, single-minded individuals who were doing the same thing as he. The only difference was, they could see.

This is one of the most fascinating true-life adventures I've encountered. Here's a man with limited resources, frost-bitten feet (from a time in the oil fields) and a definite dislike of hiking. Yet he walked more than two thousand miles over some of the roughest terrain in North America.

Why did he do it? Why spend nine months on the Trail, shivering in a three-sided lean-to or a flimsy pup tent? Why endure split fingers and bloodied knees?

Because, for Bill Irwin, the *journey* was as important as the destination. The riches were not atop Mt. Katahdin in central Maine, but rather in that first step taken each morning. It was picking himself up after tripping for the millionth time. It was sharing his fire, his candy, and his testimony with a scruffy thru-hiker somewhere in Georgia.

For Bill Irwin, each day on the Appalachian Trail was a promise kept. To God. To himself. To the hundreds of thousands of people who read about him in their newspapers or saw him interviewed on TV.

For Bill Irwin, each step was a victory.

But the tale is his to tell. Unique characters, exciting adventures, and powerful, life-changing insights are still ahead in *Blind Courage*.

Wayman R. Spence, M.D.
Chairman, WRS Publishing

The Appalachian Trail

LEGEND

① **Springer Mountain, Georgia:** March 8, 1990, the journey begins.

② **Hawk Mountain, Georgia:** Bill and Orient camp at Hawk Mountain Shelter.

③ **Neels Gap, Georgia:** Bill downsizes his pack and orders new hiking boots.

④ **Hog Pen Gap, Georgia:** Bill survives hypothermia with the help of two hikers.

⑤ **Hot Springs, North Carolina:** Bill takes a weekend to rest and give interviews to the press.

⑥ **Erwin, Tennessee:** Bill slips down the side of a mountain.

⑦ **Near Tennessee-Virginia state line:** A bear temporarily slows progress.

⑧ **Damascus, Virginia:** Anna Vail falls, breaking her leg.

⑨ **Harper's Ferry, West Virginia:** The Orient Express reaches the psychological halfway point.

⑩ **Turner's Gap, Maryland:** After missing a shelter, Bill and Orient spend the night in a boulder field.

⑪ **Duncannon, Pennsylvania:** Orient gets another checkup.

⑫ **Eastern Pennsylvania:** Bill falls in a rock field and cracks a rib.

⑬ **Southern New York:** A three-day rest at Graymoor Monastery refreshes the hikers.

⑭ **Silver Hill Cabin, Connecticut:** Orient is mistaken for a bear.

⑮ **The White Mountains, New Hampshire:** Rocks, rain, wind and fierce cold make life miserable.

⑯ **Mt. Katahdin, Maine:** Bill climbs Mt. Katahdin.

⑰ **Bigelow Mountain, Maine:** Bill and Orient spend several days alone in a ranger's cabin.

⑱ **Abol Bridge, Maine:** Bill and Orient complete their journey.

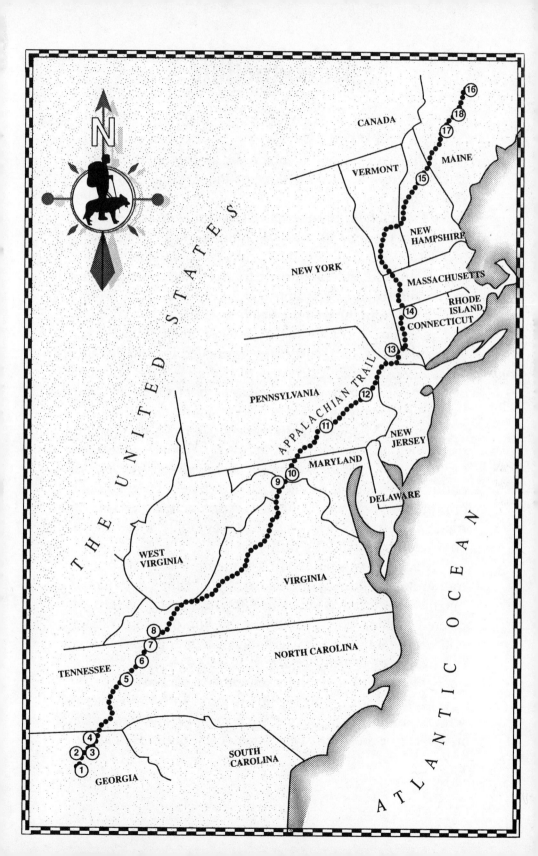

Introduction

Bill Irwin's story is not only a story of faith and determination, but also a story of the Appalachian Trail. The longest, continuously marked hiking trail in the world, the A.T. stretches unbroken for 2,168 miles from Springer Mountain, Georgia, to Mt. Katahdin in northern Maine.

The A.T. follows the peaks and valleys of the Appalachian Mountains through fourteen states, each unique in its culture and geography. Unlike other trails, which developed from the routes of Native Americans, explorers and pioneers, most of the A.T. was created where no footpath had existed before. It was created for people who want to view spectacular scenery and accept the physical challenge of scaling rugged mountains, not for easy walking from one place to another.

Benton MacKaye (pronounced muh-KYE) is often mentioned as the father of the A.T. His article in the October 1921 *Journal of the American Institute of Architects* outlined his vision for a linear park, "a series of recreational communities throughout the Appalachian chain of mountains from New England to Georgia, these to be connected by a walking trail."

MacKaye was not the first to mention a "grand trunk" trail stretching through the eastern Appalachian ridgelands, but his words gave substance to the dream. MacKaye offered a plan, which became a rallying point for others with a similar interest. It was a staggering proposal, but one that was almost fully realized by 1937 — only sixteen years after MacKaye expressed his vision in print.

Much of the credit for this belongs to Myron Avery, who became chairman of the Appalachian Trail Conference in 1931. For the next twenty-one years, until his death in

1952, Avery worked tirelessly to translate the dream into reality. By 1936, Avery had pushed a measuring wheel over every step of the proposed and constructed route from Maine to Georgia, becoming the first "two-thousand miler" on the A.T.

Today, the A.T. stands as a unique experiment in cooperation between people and government. The Trail passes through national parks and forests as well as state parks, forests, game lands and local jurisdictions. While the federal government is still acquiring the protected corridor lands along the Trail, the lion's share of Trail maintenance is done by volunteers in scores of state and local hiking clubs. In a recent year, some forty-five hundred men and women contributed more than one hundred thousand hours of work on the Trail and adjacent lands.

Because of the A.T.'s length and location along the populous eastern seaboard, two-thirds of the people in the United States live within a day's drive of the Trail. It is less than two hours by car from Philadelphia, Washington, D.C., and New York City. On clear nights, the lights of Manhattan can be seen from portions of the Trail.

In other states, the A.T. snakes through remote areas where the sights and sounds of civilization are rare. For a hundred miles in Maine, the Trail does not cross a paved road.

At times, the sense of isolation can be overpowering, despite the fact that hundreds of thousands of people set foot on the A.T. every year. Some are day-hikers out for a short walk, seeking the inner renewal that comes from even a brief encounter with nature. Others are weekenders, forsaking the city and the humdrum grind of their workaday world for the privilege of being awed by a sunrise or drenched by a thunderstorm. Others are thru-hikers, a unique band of men and women who set out to walk the entire Trail from one end to the other in a single hiking season. They carry their supplies on their backs, sleep where they want to, and enjoy a camaraderie rarely found in this modern, impersonal world.

Their reasons for taking four to six months from "real life" to walk from Maine to Georgia are as varied as their backgrounds and occupations. All who hike the Trail today are beneficiaries of the dreams — and calluses — of many thousands of people who have invested something of themselves to create and maintain this "tunnel through time."

In the later years of Benton MacKaye's life, he described the threefold purpose of the A.T. as 1) to walk, 2) to see, and 3) to see what you see. Bill Irwin *couldn't* "see what he was seeing" in the usual sense, when he and his dog guide, Orient, hiked the A.T. during eight months of 1990. But his recollection of events, people, and places on the A.T. may help others see something of the Trail — and perhaps something of themselves — that they might never otherwise discover.

Chapter One

Almost the End

The night of November 4, 1990, the radio weatherman told listeners to cherish memories of fall, because a cold front was due in that night. Just before I fell asleep, I heard it arrive — and a cold front in Maine is something to be reckoned with.

It was a fitting prelude to the events of the next day.

During the night, sleet began to pelt the tin roof of the lean-to that Dave, Orient — my dog guide[1] — and I were sharing. By morning, every rock and root outside was covered with a layer of ice.

Dave and I were hiking this stretch of the Appalachian Trail together, and I could tell he was worried about the challenges that lay ahead. We'd have to make at least a dozen river crossings in the next few days, and that would be difficult, even for a sighted person.

For me and Orient, it'd be next to impossible. For the thousandth time, I asked myself what a blind man was doing trying to walk twenty-one hundred miles along a trail from Georgia to Maine.

Next morning, I slipped and fell three times just walking the thirty yards to the creek to get water. Any other day on the Trail, I would have been content to wait in the lean-to for the weather to improve. But now, if the weather changed, it would be for the worse. Every day off the Trail

---

[1] "Dog guide" is the generic term for dogs that are trained to guide the blind. There are at least half a dozen organizations in the United States that train dog guides for the blind. The Seeing Eye is the oldest.

was a wasted day now that we were getting so close to the end. And with Dave along for this stretch, I had a pair of eyes besides Orient's to rely on, and someone to talk to about decisions that could be critical along the Trail.

We started our climb over Moxie Bald Mountain in freezing rain that turned to snow as we ascended. A quarter of a mile from the top, we encountered steeply slanted rock faces covered with three inches of snow. There was no way either Orient or I could scale them. We backtracked and took a blue-blazed by-pass[2] that we had decided against earlier that day. I had tried to stick to the white-blazed Trail[3] all the way, taking the blue-blazed Trail only when necessary. I guessed today the blue-blazed Trail *was* necessary.

We made only 5.3 miles that day and spent the night in the Moxie Bald Lean-to. Next morning, I broke my no-caffeine rule and started the day with a double hot chocolate fortified with a heaping teaspoon of instant coffee. For the first time since March, I had an intense desire just to finish the hike so I could stop hurting and go home.

But God wasn't through with me yet.

Dave and I set out soon after drinking the hot chocolate, with fifteen miles to go to the small town of Monson. With an early start and plenty of luck, we hoped to make it all the way that day.

Two and a half miles later, after we forded the knee-deep outlet of Bald Mountain Pond, my feet turned to ice. I had to stop to thaw them out. Dave boiled water for hot cocoa, and I spent an hour rubbing my feet, trying to get them warm enough to let me walk without pain.

We reached the confluence of Bald Mountain Stream and the West Branch of the Piscataquis River late in the afternoon. Two days of rain and snow had swollen the waters to a torrent that we could hear from a distance.

The sun and the temperature were both on their way down, so there was no time to waste. We sat on the bank, took off our socks, rolled our long underwear up as far as

---

[2] Blue blazes indicate side trails and, occasionally, an alternate route.
[3] White blazes indicate the actual A.T.

it would go, and put our boots back on for the crossing. Dave said the river was divided into three branches, each about thirty feet wide. Although the current was swift, they appeared fordable. I sure hoped so, because I could hear the roar of the rapids not far downstream, where three bodies of water joined together.

I took Orient's harness off and told him to find his way across. He was a strong swimmer, so I knew he could make it on his own.

"See you on the other side, boy," I said, and stepped into the icy stream. With arms linked and packs unbuckled in case we had to shed them in a hurry, Dave and I inched our way across the first thirty-foot span of water. We moved slowly, one step at a time, using our hiking sticks for stability and trying to place our boots against a rock on the bottom before taking each step. The water was knee-deep, but we reached a marshy island without incident.

Halfway across the next section, waist-deep in the strong current, Dave suddenly lost his footing and fell into the water. I could hear him sputtering and thrashing, trying to reach the next island. An instant later, I was swept off my feet and carried downstream.

I went completely under, then bobbed up, lurching and clawing through the current, trying to make it across with my pack, but ready to abandon it if I had to. Meanwhile, Dave had reached the shore. I heard him yelling something, but couldn't tell what it was. The next few seconds were pure instinct and adrenaline.

I was making no headway going toward Dave's voice; the current was too strong. In desperation, I went to the bottom of the stream and tried to pull myself along with my hands, because my feet weren't getting any traction.

When I bobbed up for a gasp of air, Dave would keep talking to me, trying to direct me towards the shore, until my head went back under the water. I felt I was slipping

further and further downstream each time I came up for air,
and the rapids were nearby.

Finally, after a few minutes that seemed like hours, I
thought I was close enough to grab Dave's outstretched
hand. I reached out but couldn't find it. The bank sloped up
steeply, and I knew I couldn't make it up alone. I started
slipping under again, thrashing about for Dave's hand,
when all of a sudden I hit a branch. I grabbed it, tight!

Most people would call the presence of the branch a
coincidence. I call it something else.

Once I grabbed the branch, I was able to find Dave's
hand with my free hand, and he helped me up. I was on the
island. Not far below, the roar of the rapids chilled me more
than the water had.

Orient, who had crossed safely, quickly came alongside
me. He was shaking, too, not from the cold, but from fear.

The final section of the stream was waist-deep again,
but calm, and we emerged on the other side, numb with
cold and badly in need of a campsite. We were amazed and
thankful to still have our packs, but there was no time now
to change into dry clothes. We had to get moving. I figured
we had an hour until dark and less than that before
hypothermia would begin to play its strange tricks on our
minds. I asked Dave to look for a level place where we
could set up the tent.

We struggled up a long ridge for half an hour, then
found an open spot in the thick woods. Numb fingers
slowed the process of pitching the tent, but minutes before
dark, we were inside, with water boiling on the stove.
Orient stretched out between us and gave a big sigh.

Still shivering in our sleeping bags, Dave and I talked
about the river and wondered how close we had come to
being completely swept away. We kept going back over the
crossing, describing our reactions and wondering what else
we could have done. If our packs had been lost, we would

have been miles from help without food or protection from the cold.

We didn't say anything for awhile, then Dave asked, "How are we going to make it the rest of the way?"

I said, "I don't know."

That was the first time I seriously considered ending the hike. By continuing, I was putting not only my life and Orient's in jeopardy, but also that of a friend.

As I lay there thinking, it seemed a century since I had begun this journey. But I knew that it had been only eight months.

Chapter Two

Getting It All Together

Eight months earlier, on March 8, 1990, I had been lying in bed listening to the rain gurgle through the downspout outside my motel room in Dahlonega, Georgia. The TV weatherman in Atlanta was saying something about this being the wettest March in seventy years.

At eight o'clock, I made myself get up.

For nearly four months I had been preparing to hike the Appalachian Trail, but now there seemed to be a barrage of unimportant details to keep me from plunging into the curtain of water falling outside. I rearranged my pack for the hundredth time, made a phone call to a friend back home and, after hanging up, felt like a kid going to camp for the first time. A few minutes later, as I stood in the shower, hot water and soap took on the feeling of luxuries rather than necessities.

Orient woke up long enough to eat his breakfast, then went back to sleep next to his canvas pack. Inside it were seventeen pounds of dog food, his grooming tools, a couple of plastic bowls, and some leather booties I'd made to protect his feet. As far as Orient was concerned, this was just another day. Knowing me as well as he did, he figured we weren't going anywhere until the rain let up. After he yawned and stretched his legs, I asked him if he wanted to go for a little walk.

Rain or not, I knew this had to be the day. It was the third anniversary of my sobriety — an almost unimaginable milestone in the life of someone who had spent most of his forty-nine years as an alcoholic. A part of me inside had been dry now for a thousand days, so maybe it didn't matter if the rest of me was about to get very wet.

Finally, about nine o'clock, Orient and I climbed into my friend Marvin's truck and headed for the Trail head at Springer Mountain.

We drove and drove, and I began to get concerned. A drive that should have taken less than thirty minutes dragged on for an hour. It gave me a lot of time to think — exactly what I didn't need to be doing. I was already on an emotional roller coaster. That morning, I was going to step out of a life which was familiar and physically comfortable into one where almost everything was unknown. I kept telling myself I was ready to hit the Trail.

The problem was finding it.

The directions we'd been given at a local gas station didn't match those from the general store. The net result was a circular route that took us nowhere. Marvin got frustrated, Orient got a lot of sleep, and I got worried.

If we couldn't find the beginning of the Appalachian Trail in a truck, how was I, a blind man, supposed to find my way to Maine on foot? But an hour and a half after leaving the motel, Marvin stopped on a Forest Service Road and said, "This is it." He assured me that we were directly in front of a tree marked with a single white paint stripe, two inches wide and six inches long.

I had to take his word for it.

For the next 2,168 miles, those white blazes would mark the route of the Appalachian Trail — if we didn't get lost. That was a real possibility, since I couldn't see the blazes and Orient didn't know what they were.

Before the pickup was out of earshot, I realized that I'd left my aluminum hiking pole in the back. Oh, me!

Somewhere along the Trail maybe I could find a stick to use for probing and stability.

I tried to shift my heavy pack to a comfortable position. My boots felt too tight. My shorts felt too small. I naively hoped things would get better. Regardless, it was too wet and cold to stand around worrying about it.

"Orient, forward."

The leather harness tightened under the fingers of my left hand as Orient took his first steps on the Trail. He seemed hesitant and uncertain about where we were going. Within ten yards, he had stopped at a large rock lying in the path. I kicked it with my boot to let him know I was aware of the obstacle and gave him the command, "Hop-up," which means "Keep going straight ahead." If he stopped for every rock on the A.T., they could expect us in Maine sometime around the turn of the century.

Of course, Orient was doing exactly what he was trained to do in the city — stop whenever he encountered an obstacle more than two inches high. It was great for curbs and steps, but obviously would not work out here. The next time he stopped for a rock, I verbally reprimanded him. Then, when he ignored one of similar size, I rewarded him with praise.

He was just getting the hang of it when I tripped over a rock he had passed by. Believe me, falling down with eighty pounds on my back was a different experience than stubbing my toe on a curb in the city. Orient stood still and whined as I struggled to right myself and get up out of the mud.

For Orient, my fall represented failure. He was supposed to prevent things like that from happening. It hadn't been his fault, but I didn't know how to tell him it was all right. We both had a lot of things to learn and the only way to do it was to keep on walking.

A few months before, all I knew about the Appalachian Trail was that it existed, and that part of it ran through my home state of North Carolina. Now I had declared my intention to hike the entire distance from Georgia to Maine during the next six months. My preparation consisted of four days in class and six miles on the Trail in Virginia during Warren Doyle's Appalachian Trail Institute.

The Institute is a crash course designed to help prospective thru-hikers[1] learn all they need to know to successfully hike the Trail. It had been a very helpful five days, but now the theory was being tested in the real world. Warren, a veteran of seven thru-hikes, had been guarded but encouraging about my chances of making it all the way.

He had left me with one strongly delivered word of advice: "Don't go alone with just Orient to guide you."

He had good reason to say that. A lot of people think that when Orient and I cross a street, he sees the green light or the little "walk" symbol and leads me across. The fact is that Orient is colorblind and doesn't have any idea what the walk symbol means. He is trained to stop me when we come to a curb. It's my job to listen to the traffic and be aware of which way it is moving. When it begins to move parallel to us, I give Orient the command to go forward and he leads us across the street, unless there is danger.

Other people have the idea that I can tell Orient, "Let's go to the bank, boy," and he'll guide us right to the teller window. If we go to the bank or anywhere else, I must know the route and tell Orient where to make his turns. His job is to guide me safely around people and obstacles along the way. A dog guide is trained to go where he is told to go by his blind master.

So the obvious question that leapt to mind was, how could I possibly tell Orient where to go on the Trail when I didn't know myself? It would have been nice if I could have shown Orient the first white blaze on a tree in Georgia and said, "See this, boy? Atta good boy! Now follow the white blazes until we get to Maine."

---

[1]Someone who hikes the full length of the A.T. in one season.

Within half an hour of being on the Trail, my clothing that wasn't wet from the rain was soaked with perspiration. Even though the temperature was in the high thirties, it felt like a sauna under my rain jacket while I was moving. But a five-minute break quickly reduced me to shivering cold. I couldn't figure out why my miracle-fabric jacket wasn't doing a better job of dispelling the moisture and regulating my body temperature. One of my first-day conclusions was that this material wasn't made for people who perspired the way I did.

By early afternoon, I had arrived at the Hawk Mountain Shelter, a three-sided wooden structure with a plank floor and sloping roof. The shelter offered protection from the rain, even though the wind seemed to whip directly into its open side. After listening to my cassette tape Trail guide, I thought I had covered 7.6 miles from the summit of Springer Mountain. "Not bad," I told myself, "for only four hours of hiking."

Since the next shelter was some nine miles away, I decided to call it a day, hang my cotton T-shirt and shorts up to dry and crawl into my sleeping bag to get warm.

In spite of the hardships of that first day, my entry into a taped journal that evening sounded optimistic:

"I believe I'm going to be able to beat the pace of eight miles a day in this first four hundred miles. If it's no steeper than it was today, it really won't be that bad. I'll probably get up early in the morning and head out and make the nine miles to Gooch Gap Shelter fairly early in the day."

Orient ate almost nothing that night, and I was surprised when he didn't snuggle close to my sleeping bag to try and stay warm. We had never done anything like this before, and I knew he was confused. It wouldn't do much good to try and explain it to him, so I just hoped that in a few days he would get accustomed to the Trail and begin to enjoy it.

With any luck at all, I might do the same.

After a restless night during which my feet never did get warm, I experienced the misery of having to emerge from a cozy sleeping bag and don a cold, clammy T-shirt and shorts. It was a feeling I immediately disliked and came to dread. Fortunately, there was no one else in the shelter to hear my moans.

The second day on the Trail quickly dispelled my optimism of the night before. Rain continued throughout the day, making the Trail several inches deep in rushing water. On the uphill climbs, the water struck my boots, cascaded up over my ankles, and often sent a spray of water into my face. Going downhill, I got the same thing from behind.

By 4:30 in the afternoon, after a full day of hiking, I had not reached Gooch Gap Shelter. My legs quivered and I fell frequently, often pulling Orient down with me. Almost everything in my backpack was soaked, and it felt at least twenty pounds heavier. Orient was even beginning to limp, so I forgot about reaching the shelter and pitched my tent beside a stream.

We had averaged less than one mile an hour during the day, and my knees were bloodied from several falls on the rocky terrain. In addition, I realized that instead of making nearly eight miles the day before, I might have miscalculated my starting point and hiked only four miles.

I examined Orient that evening and discovered an open sore under his front leg where the pack strap had rubbed him raw. After treating him with salve, I attempted to cook dinner but was unable to light any of my wet matches. Trail mix, peanut butter, and cold water made up the evening meal. Again, Orient barely touched his food.

I had figured there would be days like this — but I hadn't expected them to start so soon.

During the Institute, Warren had discussed not only the physical challenges of thru-hiking the A.T., but the

psychological ones as well. He said the only way to make
it was to keep thinking positively about every experience.

"When you're wet and cold after hiking all day in the
rain," he told us, "tell yourself that the water aquifers are
being replenished and the streams and springs will have an
abundant supply."

At the moment, that thought didn't seem too consoling,
and I couldn't imagine thirst ever being a problem. Even
so, I tried to look on the bright side. Quitting wasn't in my
vocabulary, even after an exhausting day and a cold dinner.
I knew exactly how far it was to Mt. Katahdin in Maine but
refused to let myself think about it. I had hiked a few miles
that day and would do the same again tomorrow.

I rubbed Orient's head, told him he was a good boy,
and slid into my sleeping bag next to him. We were
definitely a team because there was no way I could be out
here without him. Even though he was a working dog, we
shared a strong relationship of love. He was already asleep,
but he managed a little groan to let me know he might still
have a slight interest in being my friend.

The sound of the rain overpowered the rushing of the
creek nearby. It was a noisy kind of quiet, very relaxing
from the inside of a dry tent. For the past thirty-six hours,
I had not encountered a single human being and had heard
only one man-made sound, a distant airplane engine. The
solitude was refreshing, giving me a chance to think and
pray in a way I had never done before.

I awoke refreshed and ready to conquer the Trail, but
breaking camp in the rain subdued my enthusiasm. By
afternoon, my mood was lower than ever. After three days
of hauling my overweight pack up and down steep
mountains and helping an exhausted Orient over the rocks,
I was asking God, "Why did You want to send a peace-
loving, quiet blind man like me out here?"

Another thing Warren had told us at the Institute was
that, of the fifteen hundred people who set out to hike the

entire A.T. any year, fewer than ten percent would make it. Some would run out of time or money. Others would suffer physical injuries or illness that would end their hike. Many more would discover that their reason for beginning was not strong enough to keep them going the entire distance.

I knew I had a good reason — the best one I could imagine — for being on the Trail. God had put me here.

But why?

Why, indeed?

Chapter Three

Blinding Reality

The answer to the "why" began a long time ago. It had more to do with the blindness that afflicted my soul than with my physical blindness. Nevertheless, my physical blindness is what intrigues many people.

When people ask, "Can you see anything at all?" I reply that I have some light perception. If I'm in a dark room and someone turns on a light, I'm aware of it. I can distinguish day from night, noon from dusk, bright sunlight from shade. I cannot see shapes or images.

My vision problems began in 1968 when I was working eighteen hours a day at three jobs. From 5:00-8:00 a.m., I worked as a medical technologist in a Birmingham, Alabama, hospital. From 8:00 a.m. till noon, I taught high-school chemistry in a private school to pay my children's tuition. After that, I worked until midnight in my own clinical laboratory, which was just getting off the ground.

One morning while teaching chemistry, I wrote a formula on the blackboard. When I looked back at it from a different angle, the formula was gone. It took me a few minutes to discover that I could see it with my right eye, but not with my left.

That afternoon, I asked Walter Ford, a medical doctor and my partner in the laboratory, to look at my eye. After a brief examination, he promptly canceled his afternoon appointments and hustled me off to an ophthalmologist.

Following a thorough examination and further tests, the eye doctor and five of his associates unanimously concluded that I had malignant melanoma in my left eye. Because the fast-spreading cancer was located so near the brain, they decided to remove my left eye as soon as possible. They also told me as gently as they could that I probably would not live longer than three months at the most. I was stunned.

Mentally, I knew that young men sometimes had cancer, but I wasn't ready to die at age twenty-eight. I had a wife, three children under the age of eight, and a whole life to live.

All of a sudden I found myself on death row.

Dying was not something I was remotely interested in, nor was I prepared for it, mentally, emotionally, or spiritually. From what I knew of God at that time, He certainly would not be pleased with my lifestyle. I didn't want to have to explain it to Him any time soon.

Meeting God face-to-face struck me as being a lot like confronting my father the time my friend Dan Davis and I took my parents' car. Dan and I were both about twelve and looking for some excitement in our little hometown of Leeds, Alabama, so we went for a spin when my parents were out for the evening. We found more excitement than we wanted when my mother and father arrived home before we did.

I can still remember every detail. My father, a prominent surgeon in town, approached the car after we drove in, and told Dan that he "was excused" and could go home. Dad then took me to my room and laid into me with his belt. I had welts on my backside for a week from that whipping. If the Almighty was anywhere near as stern as my father had been, the longer I could put off facing Him, the better.

For eight weeks after my eye was removed, I tried to get my business affairs in order while living the pleasure-saturated life of a man with no tomorrow. The few moral rules I might have followed before didn't seem to matter any longer since I was about to be ejected from the game anyway.

I probably would have killed myself with dissipation if my diseased eye hadn't been making the rounds of some of the nation's top pathologists. One alert physician among them examined the eye tissue and came back with a dissenting opinion. His tests revealed not cancer, but an unnamed degenerative disease. According to him, I was not about to die, and the worst thing I faced was a fifty-fifty chance of losing the sight in my right eye.

I was so relieved by this reprieve from death that the loss of my left eye seemed a small matter. I had even odds on avoiding further problems, and never considered total blindness a real possibility.

Most importantly, I wasn't going to have to face death — or God — in the near future, and that was just fine with me.

Overnight, my emotions went back up as far as they had gone down. I plunged back into my workaholic lifestyle as if nothing had happened.

One morning five years later, my secretary at the laboratory placed the usual steaming mug of hot coffee on my desk. When I glanced down to pick it up, I could see only half the mug. I knew exactly what was happening, and it scared me to death.

This time, the ophthalmologists gave my condition a name, *chorioretinitis*. They described it as a hereditary autoimmune disease and told me that laser treatments might slow its progress, but that I would eventually become completely blind. The best they could do was give me the treatments and try to buy me a little time.

My business had grown from two to twenty-five employees, but I had an ongoing cash-flow problem, since I was trying to pay back a sizable loan. Knowing that my days as a clinical chemist were numbered, I sold the business and stayed on with the company that bought it.

One of the most frightening things for me about going blind was the prospect of being unable to work. Another was being single.

At the time, work was a major escape from the troubled relationships in my life. My first marriage had failed in 1971, and my second ended shortly after my vision problem recurred in 1973. Being single held about the same interest for me as dying, since somehow I equated true happiness with being married. Blindness didn't seem like something that would enhance my chances of finding a happy relationship with someone in the future.

Things weren't a lot better for me with my three kids. A man once described parenting by saying, "For the first twelve years you can't do anything wrong, and for the next twelve you can't do anything right." If that was true, I was in real trouble, because I hadn't done many things right during their *first* twelve years. Now they were headed into the turbulent teens while being shuffled back and forth between their mother and me. Our attempt at remarriage had ended after three months, and we all seemed trapped into repeating the same patterns of conflict I had grown up with.

Part of that was the result of my formula for dealing with any problem — ignore it or repress it, but never, ever, discuss it.

As my sight gradually deteriorated, I alternated between periods of active preparation for blindness and deep depression over it. For a time, I studied Braille and practiced cooking and functioning at home in the evenings with all the lights out. Then there were the months when I came home from work, slumped into my easy chair, and drank until I fell asleep. I never missed a day on the job, but I rarely spent an hour after work without a drink in my hand.

The combination of the degenerative disease and the laser treatments may have produced the bizarre visual images that presented themselves. People's teeth would seem to be several inches long, emerging from distorted faces. The beautiful world I loved was becoming twisted and misshapen. I could still read with a powerful, lighted magnifying glass, but it required greater effort each day.

With all this, I was determined to keep driving as long as I could, even after it became dangerous. It took a near-tragedy to wake me up. One day in 1974, I drove over a fire hydrant without ever seeing it. Later, I realized that the hydrant was just about the size of a two-year-old child. It frightened me so much I voluntarily turned in my driver's license, even though I mourned my resulting loss of independence.

By 1976, my sight was completely gone.

At that time, I was working as the personnel director for a clinical laboratory in Burlington, and trying to deal with the new limitations in my life. I had learned to use a white cane, which gave me a degree of mobility. But I hated the attention it directed toward me. As a result, I began spending almost all my time outside of work at home. Increased alcohol consumption and limited physical activity caused my weight and my blood pressure to go up dramatically.

For nearly two years, I spent most of my evenings sitting at home being depressed over what I had lost and would never have again. I didn't even bother to turn the lights on because darkness seemed to be the world in which I was destined to spend the rest of my life.

The word "depressing" used as a verb describes what I was doing during that time. I sat at home choosing to be depressed. I've come to see my attitude and my actions during that time as deliberate choices, not conditions forced on me.

At work and in society, I felt like a freak, with one glass eye and another that was useless. My white cane seemed nothing more than a signal to let everyone know that I was less of a person than they were. It was a miserable existence, and I was the most pathetic part of it.

People began treating me differently and I hated it. Often, when I ate with friends in a restaurant, the waitress would take everyone's order but mine, then ask someone at my table, "And what will *he* have?" Usually, I would look at her and say, "If you'll ask *him,* he'll tell you what he wants."

Just because I couldn't read the menu didn't mean I was incapable of ordering for myself.

What was just as annoying was that people began speaking louder when they talked to me. Did they think I was deaf, too?

Helen Keller said that, "not blindness, but the attitude of the seeing to the blind is the hardest burden to bear." I agree.

I was too wrapped up in myself to realize how all this was affecting my children. Marianne, my only daughter, kept her emotions pretty well bottled up inside. Billy acted out his frustrations by leaving home on a regular basis. Jeff, the youngest, was embarrassed by my blindness. If he missed the bus in the morning, he had to take a taxi to school because I was unable to drive him. I never went to his football games because it seemed foolish to sit in the stands when I couldn't see him play.

Blindness accentuated the problems I had always tried to gloss over before. The more I sought freedom in alcohol and self-gratifying behavior, the more I became bound by the chains of addiction. Broken relationships, wounded pride, and a loss of independence deepened the depression which settled over our house like a thick gloom.

Fortunately, I had one friend who never quit getting on my case about becoming a recluse. He kept after me, kept trying to get me to go places with him, but I wouldn't have any of it. I'd gotten to the point where I no longer went anywhere but work.

Finally, he came over and said, "You can sit here for the rest of your life and wallow in alcohol if you want to, but you're going to do it by yourself. I'm not going to have anything to do with it." And then he left. I sat there and thought about what he said for a week. Finally, I called him.

"Uh... how about if we go to dinner tonight?"

I'd finally become sick of sitting around feeling sorry for myself. This was no way to live. But if I wanted things to change, something told me I was the only one who could make it happen. Since I couldn't alter the fact that I was blind, I decided to pull myself up by my own bootstraps and live in spite of it.

After that, I planned social activities when it looked like I was going to be alone, especially when the children weren't with me. At the same time, I starting taking advantage of social services for the blind, learning cane travel, learning mobility and orientation. All of this happened a couple of years before I got my first dog guide. With my friend's help, I had finally broken my destructive pattern.

It seemed that I had been prepared for adversity from an early age. As a child, my parents had drilled into me the belief that we Irwins were better than other people. According to them, Irwins didn't fail and we didn't ever quit. If I had to live without sight for the rest of my life, I was going to do everything I could not to *act* as if I were blind.

My decision in 1978 to get a Seeing Eye dog was difficult, because it required a significant commitment on my part. The dog and I would be together twenty-four hours a day, seven days a week, until one of us became disabled or died. That sounded a lot like marriage to me, and I was already zero for three in that type of relationship. Besides, I couldn't imagine pursuing my chosen lifestyle with a dog around all the time. I could just picture asking some lady to excuse me from the table at a restaurant because I had to take my dog to the bathroom. It seemed like a social detriment that would be hard to overcome.

I couldn't have been more wrong.

The Seeing Eye training facility in Morristown, New Jersey, performed the dual role of training people while matching us with an appropriate dog guide. The dogs had all spent most of their first year with a 4-H family, learning basic obedience and manners. Then they went to the training facility for twelve weeks' training before we met them. Then we had four weeks together in a training program that was thorough, personal, and demanding. We were taught how to handle our dogs, as well as the importance of establishing a relationship with them based on mutual love and respect. We left with a commitment to keep our dogs healthy and well-groomed, to walk them at least two miles a day, and to stand up for our legal right to take them into all public places.

After I got my first dog, Jorie, the physical and mental aspects of my life took an immediate turn for the better. We began walking the eight miles round trip to work every day. In public settings, I was amazed at the number of people who stopped to talk to Jorie and later got around to asking him, "And who's this guy with you?"

My feeling of being conspicuous disappeared when I walked with a dog. He could guide me around obstacles without my having to touch and identify them with the cane. He strengthened my resolve that if I had to be blind, I was going to do everything I could *not* to appear that way.

My dog enabled me to function well in the business world, too. My job in sales training, and later as an independent consultant in the area of toxicology, involved a great deal of travel and social interaction. My dog was always an asset in every situation. Well, almost always.

One notable exception occurred on a bitter winter day, when Jorie and I were walking to work in Burlington. The cold wind hurt my eye, so I pulled my stocking cap all the way down over my face. Within two blocks, a policeman stopped me and threatened to give me a ticket for creating a traffic hazard. He explained that, when the people in cars saw me striding along with no apparent way to see, they slowed down to gawk. I didn't want a ticket, and I didn't want anyone to get hurt, so I pulled up the hat and let everyone get to work on time.

When Jorie developed hip dysplasia, he could walk on level ground but he could no longer climb steps. I began carrying him up and down stairs, and people started staring again. Eventually, Jorie had to be retired, and I got Sailor, my second dog.

The working life of a dog guide is usually from five to ten years. The bond that develops in that time between dog and master is difficult to describe. It goes beyond friendship and affection to include mutual admiration and respect. A dog guide is motivated by unconditional love, and a person can't receive that without wanting to return it in some way.

When Sailor had to be retired, he went to live with another family. Then I got Orient.

Orient, like my other two dogs, came from The Seeing Eye. Their method of training dogs is built primarily around verbal reward and reprimand. Every desirable act is followed by enthusiastic praise, "Atta good boy (or girl)!" while each mistake is greeted with the Swiss word *pfui!* (fwee), an expression of extreme displeasure. (Of course, when I say it, it sounds more like "Phooey!") The dog's natural desire to please its master, not physical punishment, is the basis of its learning.

Perhaps the most incredible result of this type of training is that the dog is taught to think and make decisions, not merely to obey. For instance, the trainer will tell the dog to go forward across an empty street just as another trainer rounds the corner in a car. Through verbal reward or reprimand, the dog is taught to disobey its master's command if obedience will bring harm. The result is what The Seeing Eye calls "intelligent disobedience."

I vividly remember my first meeting with Orient, and the anxiety I felt about it. When a blind person meets a prospective dog guide, the introduction is made in a quiet room where only the trainer, the dog, and the prospective owner are present. The blind person is seated across the room from the trainer and dog, then told to call the dog by name in a friendly voice while clapping his hands together. The trainer releases the dog who, hopefully, comes to greet the new owner. I knew that frequently, the dog would make a big circle and go right back to the trainer, with whom he had a strong bond.

As I sat in the room waiting to meet Orient, I wondered what he would do. All my apprehension melted away when I called "Orient!" and clapped my hands. He bolted across the room, put both paws on my chest and began to whine and lick my face. I knew that he already liked me.

I had always marveled at the devotion of dog guides, but the first days on the Trail gave me a new admiration for Orient.

On our fourth morning in Georgia, I could feel his cold nose nudging me awake in the tent. For the first time on the Trail, I awoke to sunshine instead of rain.

Chapter Four

Life in the Slow Lane

On Sunday, March 11, 1990, the sun bathed the Trail in bright light and my spirits rose with the warmth from its rays. It was a stunningly beautiful Georgia spring day. The birds were singing and the whole world smelled fresh and clean. I remember thinking that this must be the kind of experience that drew people back to the Trail.

An early morning tumble and a broken backpack frame failed to dampen my spirits as I headed toward Neels Gap and my first taste of civilization in four days. My goal was a hot shower, a real bed, and a chance to unload some of the unnecessary items in my pack. A man I met on the Trail had lifted my pack and said, "You'll never make it to Maine with this. It must weigh ninety pounds." To me, it felt more like a hundred and ninety, but I took his word for it.

In addition to my own wet clothing and gear, I was carrying Orient's pack because abrasions had developed under both his front legs. He was still limping and seemed to be struggling with every step. I had never considered being unable to complete the hike because of an injury to him, but now that loomed as a real possibility. His pack had fit fine when we tested it before getting on the Trail, but then he hadn't been climbing mountains and carrying seventeen pounds of food. Maybe someone at Neels Gap could rework the pack so he could carry it again after he healed.

As I struggled up Big Cedar Mountain, I began to wonder about the person who called the Appalachian Trail "a footpath for those who seek fellowship with the wilderness." There was no "footpath" to this part of the hike, and a little fellowship with the wilderness went a long way with me. I had heard people say they thought Georgia was the most difficult stretch of the A.T. and now I knew why. If that were true, at least I was getting the hard part out of the way early.

This was pure mountain climbing without any level stretches in between. There wasn't time to enjoy getting to the top of a mountain before starting down again. And going downhill was the most difficult and dangerous part for me. Uphill was hard on my back, legs and lungs, but no one ever got killed falling uphill. The steep descents, on the other hand, were just plain treacherous. I had to make Orient slow down and take extra care because a slip here could spell disaster.

Each time my foot was about to hit the ground, a dozen questions ran through my mind: "What is the surface of the Trail? Is it smooth or rocky? Dry or muddy? Is it slanted to the left or right, forward or back? If I step on a rock, is it stable or loose? If it's loose, which direction is it going to move? If it's a root or branch, is it alive or rotten? Will it give or break?"

When the answer came back from my foot to my brain, I had a millisecond to make a correction and compensate for what I couldn't see. By the end of a day, I was more fatigued mentally than physically. And poor Orient must have been just as tired from trying to figure out what he was supposed to do in this new environment.

With every downhill step, my toes jammed into the front of my nine-dollar hiking boots, sending jolts of pain all the way up my legs. The man who had sold them to me had assured me there was no need to spend more than that on a pair of boots. On that Sunday morning, I would've paid big money for a pair of boots that fit.

By early afternoon, Orient and I had made only five miles and were both completely worn out. Had there been a Trail relocation since the latest Trail guide was written? According to the carved signs — which I could read with my fingers — I was still a good six miles from Neels Gap.

I decided to set up camp and string a clothesline. If nothing else, I could dry everything out and regroup for the next day. After only four days on the Trail, I was already a few miles behind schedule, and stopping early meant I wouldn't make my destination again that day. I was feeling guilty and a bit discouraged when a woman's voice said, "Hi, how's it going?"

Patty, the owner of the voice, lived near Atlanta and was returning from a day hike when she saw me camped just off the Trail. I told her how discouraged and guilty I felt, and she said, "Looks to me like you're doing the right thing, getting your stuff all dried out." She had thru-hiked the A.T. several years earlier, and assured me that it was not a sign of weakness or a waste of time. She added that I looked like a guy who was going to make it all the way to Maine.

When I told her about my plan to mail some of my gear home from Neels Gap, she told me that a lot of thru-hikers did the same thing. "Everyone starts off with an overweight pack," she said. "It takes a few days to figure out what you don't need."

We talked together for an hour or so before she went on her way. I was convinced she was an angel sent to encourage me just when I was beginning to doubt my judgment and ability to handle the Trail. She must have encouraged Orient, too, because he ate all his food that night for the first time since we started. He was so tired that he ate lying down with his muzzle stretched across the bowl. It was all he could do to lick the dog food into his mouth and chew it. I treated his sores again with antiseptic cream and checked his feet for cuts. His pads were in good shape and I hoped his energy level would pick up soon.

After dinner, I began mentally reviewing the things in my pack to decide what I didn't need. I had so many gadgets with me I couldn't believe it. If it ran on batteries, I had it. There were three tape recorders, a radio, a timer that I couldn't get to turn off at night, three knives, and a 35-mm camera so people could take pictures for my scrapbook. Surely I didn't need the air pistol, the extra CO_2 cylinders or the pellets. The pistol looked like a .357 magnum and probably weighed three pounds. I had planned to keep the mice and the raccoons away with it, but maybe Orient could just growl at them instead.

The bird-call tapes would have to go back too. I had had big educational plans for all my free time on the hike, and one of my goals was to be able to identify all the birds along the way by their songs. Maybe that would work some other time when I didn't have to carry six cassettes to do it.

I must have fallen asleep thinking about my pack, because I woke up in what seemed to be the middle of the night. The female voice from my talking watch, which I affectionately called Luanna, told me it was 7:24 p.m. I laughed and went back to sleep. This was definitely life in the slow lane.

The next morning, with the goal of reaching Neels Gap that day, I scaled Blood Mountain and promptly got lost descending the other side. I knew we were off the Trail when branches began hitting me in the face and the familiar rocky surface was replaced by crunching leaves and twigs. Orient must have taken a side trail.

We had crossed the open summit of the mountain and begun our descent while still on the Trail. It seemed reasonable to assume that if we began walking around the mountain while maintaining the same elevation, we would intersect the A.T. on one side or the other. We made a ninety-degree turn to the left and, within a few minutes, we found the Trail. Orient seemed quite pleased with himself for getting us back on track.

By early afternoon, I was leaning on the counter at the Walasi-Yi Center at Neels Gap. What happened during the next twenty-four hours did more to encourage me than the events of any other single day on the entire hike.

When Jeff and Dorothy Hansen asked how they could help me, my first concern was Orient's pack. They had some excellent dog packs in their outfitters' store, but they were very expensive. So Jeff mentioned a local woman — Karen Padgett — and said she was the only person he knew with the skill and equipment to modify Orient's heavy canvas pack. He tried to reach her by phone but, when the call went unanswered, he seemed pretty pessimistic about finding her. She was gone a great deal of the time, he said, and he didn't know if she was even in the area.

A few minutes later, Karen's husband walked right in the front door of the store. He just "happened" to be driving by and stopped in to get a cold drink. Jeff and Dorothy couldn't believe it. The man told us how to get in touch with his wife, and that evening the three of us shared a wonderful time together while she modified Orient's pack using her industrial sewing machine. She wouldn't even accept any payment for her work.

A couple of years before, I would have agreed with all the folks who describe something like that as a wonderful coincidence or with a lot of thru-hikers, who call it "Trail magic."

But since then, I had come to believe there was no such thing as coincidence — unless you redefined coincidence as "God performing a miracle while maintaining His anonymity." This was a big departure from the kind of thinking that had governed most of my life.

Jeff spent several hours with me going through my pack, helping me decide what to keep and what to send home. Some were obvious decisions, like the radio and the extra tape recorders, but other things surprised me. Jeff put each item from my pack on a scale, told me what it weighed, and asked me, "Is it worth it?"

Most of my extra weight was in ounces, not pounds. I didn't need half of what was in my first-aid kit, or the extra tube of toothpaste, or most of my backup clothing. I seemed to have an extra one of everything. My twenty-nine-tool Swiss Army knife weighed nearly a pound and could be adequately replaced by one weighing only an ounce. My metal knife, fork and spoon set gave way to a single plastic spoon.

Jeff advised me to send home all my cotton clothes and gave me several items made of polypropylene to replace them. When "polypro" gets wet, it retains body heat while allowing moisture to escape. Cotton does just the opposite, creating the perfect conditions for hypothermia. I guess that's why hikers referred to anything made of cotton as "dead man's clothes."

By the time we were through, I had eliminated twenty-six pounds of clothing and equipment. Jeff assured me it happened to almost everyone. Last hiking season alone, he had shipped more than four thousand pounds of equipment home for overloaded thru-hikers. At least now I might be able to stand still with my pack on instead of weaving around all the time.

Jeff had a great selection of quality hiking boots in his store, but none were a size fourteen. However, he agreed to order a pair for me and get them to my next mail drop. I wasn't too excited about doing another 130 miles in my low budget foot-destroyers, but at least there was hope on the horizon. Maybe after my toenails fell off, they wouldn't hurt so much.

Dorothy fixed the most delicious spaghetti dinner I'd ever eaten. When she gave some to Orient, I pretended not to notice. He gobbled the spaghetti down faster than any thru-hiker.

When we'd eaten, I did something I would do nearly every week for the next seven months. I called Carolyn Starling, the leader of my support team back in Burlington, North Carolina.

When Carolyn had agreed to take the job of coordinator for my hike, she thought that the Trail was like a paved golf cart path. She assumed it would be a matter of coordinating the food and mail, answering a few questions from friends, and handling my requests when I stopped to rest. But when I called her from Neels Gap for the first time and described my first four days, it just frightened her to death. When I gave her a "honey do" list a mile long after just five days, she realized the scope of her role.

Suddenly, in addition to her family and her full-time job, she had to keep track of all the hiking gear I was sending back, contact equipment manufacturers, and try to get several essential items to me through post offices in little Trail towns she'd never heard of. It just about overwhelmed her. She quickly saw that, without a lot of help from God, she would not be able to provide the kind of support I needed. She had had no inkling of the demands of this job — and neither had I!

That night the Hansen's children, Jamie and Christopher, gave Orient and me lots of hugs. That was better than the hot shower, the spaghetti, and the real bed. Four-year-old Christopher told me about his "wood house," an imaginary place in the sky where he put people who were very special to him. Only the people he liked a lot qualified to live in his wood house as part of his family. When he called me his "wood father," I was honored. By the time I crawled into bed that night, I felt like I'd won the grand prize on the old fifties TV show, "Queen For A Day."

Orient seemed to be feeling better and that was a big relief. He lay down next to my bed that night and nuzzled my hand a little bit when I reached down to rub his head. I was determined not to ask him to do more than he could, and to stop and rest as often as he needed to. I planned to continue carrying his pack for a couple of weeks until his sores healed, then let him build up gradually to carrying his normal load.

During the past four days, he had led me through rain and cold, walked up to his belly in rushing water, and carried a pack that rubbed him raw. He had never complained or whined except to tell me he was in pain. Without Orient, I couldn't function normally in life or be out here on the Trail. I was grateful to have him as a partner and a friend.

Chapter Five

...And Forgetting Where I Put It

Orient and I left Neels Gap on Tuesday afternoon, March 13th, a lot lighter in pack weight — and in spirit — than when we had arrived twenty-four hours earlier.

I was euphoric about all Jeff and Dorothy Hansen and Karen Padgett had done for me. I was sure it was more than coincidence that these people had been there right when I needed them so much. Jeff had almost completely rearranged my pack, gotten me out of my dangerous cotton clothing into what experienced hikers wear, and charged me practically nothing.

We all hugged when Orient and I left, and they thanked us for coming. I certainly didn't expect that kind of treatment all the way to Maine, but it left me with a strong sense that God was going to take care of us.

Orient and I started walking with about four hours of daylight remaining to cover the seven miles to our meeting place. There, we were supposed to meet Tom Reed, a freelance photographer, who had asked if he could hike along with us for a couple of days. It seemed a simple enough connection to make, even though I wasn't thrilled about attracting media attention.

We didn't make the connection that night, however, and the reasons for that were typical of how events on the Trail could quickly turn bad for me.

Several hundred yards after crossing Highway 348 at Hog Pen Gap, I remembered that I was supposed to tie a red bandana near the road to let Tom know I had passed that point. I had taken off my pack and was about to start back for the road, when a couple of hikers named John and Ed came by. They were southbound and offered to take the bandana back for me. When I asked about campsites ahead, they mentioned a nice level area about a mile up the Trail.

Twenty minutes later, Orient led me to the campsite just off the Trail. He was ready to call it a day, but first we needed water. We had drunk the two quarts I had carried from Neels Gap, and we hadn't found any more all day. I thought it ironic that, a few days earlier, I had been walking ankle-deep in water and now there was none to be found. As I took off my pack, I realized I was thirstier than I had ever been in my life.

I dropped my pack next to a campfire ring, and grabbed the fabric water bag that Jeff had thrust into it that morning. He had said it would come in handy, and it looked like he knew what he was talking about!

Orient and I headed for the stream where John and Ed had said we could find water.

It was a steep downhill descent littered with rocks and toppled trees. If there was a trail, I couldn't find it, and at the time, it didn't make any difference. I was driven by a thirst that became more urgent by the moment. I stumbled and fell most of the way to the bottom of the ravine, where I plunged my face into a gurgling stream. Orient and I drank our fill, caught our breath, and drank some more.

I filled the water bag, hoisted its twenty pounds, and wondered if we could find our campsite up on the mountain. Before descending, I had tried to take a mental fix on our location at the top, but had lost it completely in the twisting, turning scramble down the mountain. Going back up was even worse.

With Orient walking ahead, I began the ascent behind him on all fours. The precious water was a heavy burden in the thickets and branches that blocked our way. Briers sliced stinging gashes into my arms and legs, adding to the difficulties of the climb. By the time we had skirted the worst of the fallen trees and reached the top, I had no idea where we were.

During our trip down and back it had become pitch dark, limiting Orient's vision. Since I had sent my headlamp home from Neels Gap, I now had no light to help him navigate after dark. Because of this, we crisscrossed the top of the mountain several times before finding the Trail, and even then we were unable to locate the campsite. I realized how foolish I had been to leave my pack in the camp instead of right on the Trail.

I resigned myself to spending the night in the open without any food for either of us.

Worse than the lack of food, however, was the lack of shelter. Orient was wearing his fur coat — but I was clad in shorts and a T-shirt, and it was getting cold. The temperature was dropping into what felt like the low forties as the wind picked up. I knew I had to find some way of preventing too much loss of body heat, so I felt around and shoved some leaves together into a bed for the two of us. Even though the leaves were wet, I thought they might warm up with the heat from our bodies, and provide a measure of protection against the chill.

We lay down together and I was thankful that at least we had water and that it wasn't pouring rain. Still, I knew that my body was losing heat faster than it was producing it. If I became hypothermic, we were in double trouble, because the mental disorientation that hypothermia produces would prevent me from doing what was needed to survive.

Maybe my thinking had *already* become faulty, since I was lying there in a cold bed of wet leaves!

Suddenly the thought came to me, "Go find Ed and John." I remembered that the two had said they planned to camp at Hog Pen Gap, which was within two miles of where we were. I slipped Orient's harness on him, picked up the water bag, and we started on the Trail in what I hoped was the right direction. Orient put his nose to work sniffing out the way and didn't stumble at all.

When we reached the road, I blew my whistle three times, the signal for an emergency. Within a few minutes, Ed and John found us and took us to their camp. Sitting under their tarpaulin, I was shaking so hard from the cold that I could hardly hold the cup of hot tea they gave me. They said I was already dangerously beyond the first stages of hypothermia. The warm food and hot drinks they shared with me probably saved my life.

They were glad that I had brought a water bag, because they were almost out of water and there was none close by. They provided the food and shelter, and I supplied the water — just what we all needed that night to survive.

Orient's dog food was in my pack, so he ate some of our food for supper. He lapped up the noodles and oatmeal as if it were some kind of special treat. After spaghetti at Neels Gap and noodles at Hog Pen Gap, he'd want to order from the menu the next time we came to a town!

Bedtime presented another difficulty. John and Ed had their sleeping bags, but mine was with my lost pack. I gladly accepted their offer of a Mylar™ emergency blanket and wrapped up in it, huddled between the two of them. It helped, but it wasn't enough. I kept shivering so hard that the Mylar™ blanket rattled and kept us all awake. I must have sounded like a wet dog wrapped up in waxed paper.

After an hour of this, one of the guys offered to let me crawl in the sleeping bag with him. I was reluctant to do it, but I was still quite cold, and thought what a kind gesture it was for a man to share such close quarters with a total stranger. Warmth came quickly from his body heat on one side and Orient's on the other.

The whole sequence of events had been like a near-collision in a car. The sense of how narrow an escape we had had didn't come until I was safely through it. I fell asleep marveling at the fact that, when I was in desperate need, someone was there to help. I believed God had sent John and Ed, whether they knew it or not.

The next morning, Orient and I found our packs and I treated him to a double ration of dog food and some Milkbone dog "cookies." Somewhere up the Trail, there was a photographer wondering where we were. The thought crossed my mind that if he gave up and went home, that would be just fine with me. There would be other stories for him — and the less publicity for me, the better.

Jeff Hansen had told me that the grapevine among hikers on the A.T. was a more sophisticated communication network than modern media, and it was just a matter of time until everyone knew who I was and where I was on the Trail. He felt publicity was inevitable and I was going to have to get used to it and decide how to handle it. I didn't want to deal with it.

I gave Orient another "cookie." If I could get him to do all the talking, I'd have it made.

Chapter Six

Why Me, Lord?

Dealing with the media was something I had neither wanted nor prepared myself for. Before the hike, I hadn't been particularly surprised when Jim Wicker of the *Burlington Times-News* called me at home and asked if he could do a story about Orient and me — a hometown newspaper is supposed to cover local people and events that no one else would be interested in. Since I figured that general interest in my hike was somewhere between that generated by a 4-H banquet and a possible increase in garbage collection rates, it seemed natural for him to call me.

So I agreed to an interview, and on February 28, Jim came over with photographer Jack Sink. We talked for about an hour and then, since Jack wanted some pictures of me with the backpack on, Orient and I strolled around the lawn a little for the camera. Orient had no pack on and I was dressed in a sweater, cords and loafers. Whatever we looked like, it sure wasn't thru-hikers.

When Jim's story appeared on March 1, it contained one bit of information that later proved embarrassing. He said that Orient and I were planning to hike the A.T. both ways — a 4,338-mile journey. Climbing Mt. Katahdin would mark the halfway point, he wrote, after which we would immediately turn around and start back toward Georgia.

That's what I had told him; that's what I had intended in the beginning.

When my son Billy and I were sitting by the fire in my warm, dry living room in January, reading *The AT Data Book* and setting daily mileage goals, I saw no reason why I couldn't average twenty miles a day and often a lot more. Orient and I were already walking fifteen miles a day on the streets of Burlington and taking occasional day hikes in nearby Duke Forest. It'd be a piece of cake, I thought.

Initially, I planned to make Katahdin by mid-July.

After the first week on the Trail, I revised my itinerary. I don't think I ever mentioned a round-trip thru-hike again.

Jim's story also clearly stated my reason for hiking the Appalachian Trail. That made me feel good because it was the simple, unvarnished truth.

Well, actually, it wasn't quite so simple.

Hikers, reporters and people in towns along the Trail asked me frequently why on earth I wanted to hike the Appalachian Trail in the first place. It was a difficult question to answer. I was never quite sure how much of my story they wanted to hear.

My introduction to the Trail came in August, 1989. It was so subtle I almost missed it. I had been to the annual Fiddlers' Convention in Galax, Virginia, because I love mountain music. It was so much fun I called my son, Billy, to see if he and his son, Jonathan, would come for the final day. I thought we might even camp out for a night on the way home. We had never done that — my idea of roughing it was a motel with skimpy towels — and it would give us a chance to enjoy some time together.

For the first time in many years, I felt Billy and I were beginning to communicate and build a relationship. During my three children's growing-up years, I had spent almost all my time telling them what to do. I rarely asked them how they felt about anything. But things had been changing lately, and I wanted to keep the process alive.

After the Fiddlers' Convention, Billy, Jonathan and I drove down the Blue Ridge Parkway and pitched our tent in a little campground. One quiet morning while Billy and Jonathan were away from the campsite, I was thinking back over the last few years and thanking God for everything He had done in my life. In a matter of months, I had become free from alcohol and tobacco. I was now aware of a physical world to which I had been numb for most of my adult life.

And I was spiritually alive. When I told people I was born again, it was more than a cliché to me. A part of me that had been as dead as a tent peg had come to life and I knew it. It had changed my entire purpose for living.

Sitting there in that campground, I began talking to God. "Lord," I said, "I'm so grateful for all You've given me and all You've done for me. If there's ever anything I can do as a way of saying thanks to You, I want You to know I'll do it, whatever it is."

That was it. I didn't give it a second thought.

On the way home, Billy told me a little about the Appalachian Trail and his interest in hiking part of it. It sounded like a long walk to me — twenty-one hundred miles through fourteen states along the spine of the Appalachian Mountains! When he talked about the thru-hikers who tackled it all in one six-month stretch, I thought they seemed like folks who could use some Reality Therapy. An afternoon in the mountains was usually enough to satisfy *my* appetite for a wilderness experience. After that, I was ready to head home to my water bed and hot tub.

Soon I was in school preparing to be a family counselor, not a hiker, and I didn't think any more about it.

A month or two later, Billy's personal interest in the A.T. led him to write for more information about it. Since he was raising a family and going to college, he knew he wouldn't be able to hike it himself — at least not any time soon — so he kept reading the information to me.

Strangely, other stories about long-distance pilgrimages started coming my way as well, totally unsolicited. An aunt sent me an article about the Peace Pilgrim, a lady who had spent the last fifteen years of her life walking from city to city, talking about peace. Someone else sent me Terry Fox's story. Terry was the young man with one leg who had walked across Canada to raise money for the Cancer Society, but died before he finished his trip.

So gradually I began to feel compelled to do *something*, but I didn't know what. I didn't really give it much thought, although I did ask myself why people were sending me all this stuff. I thought it was great, but I didn't think any of it applied to me. At one point, I even told Billy, "I just have no interest in the Appalachian Trail. None."

When the thought first occurred that the *Lord* might want me to hike the Trail, I put it out of my mind. When the idea kept coming back, I told God He had the wrong Bill Irwin, "I'm the blind guy, remember?"

But in the weeks that followed, the Lord really burdened me with the idea of walking the A.T.

Why the A.T.? I don't know, but I never considered anyplace else. I even tried to forget about it. As the feeling got more pronounced, I once prayed, "Lord, You know I'd be *willing* to do anything for You, but You know I'm just not able to do this... don't You?"

It didn't help.

There were dozens of reasons why I was the wrong man to hike this Trail — or any trail.

At six feet, one inch and 190 pounds, I'm big, but not very coordinated. The best word for it is clumsy. The only reason I played football in high school was my size. My job as a lineman was to get in the way of other people, and fortunately, that didn't demand a lot of finesse.

And my legs are terrible. Most hikers have strong legs. I don't. After a bout with hepatitis in 1961, I had spent the better part of nine months in bed. During that time, my calf muscles had atrophied and it had taken me several weeks to learn to walk again. Those shrunken muscles never returned to their normal size.

In addition, my legs are unusually short for a man six feet tall. If you wonder who buys the trousers with the thirty-six inch waist and twenty-nine inch length that are always left on the sale table, it's me. My legs are too short for climbing mountains and my muscles are too weak.

God should have known that already.

Then there are my feet. When I was fifteen, I left home abruptly, under cover of darkness, to seek my fortune in the Texas oil fields. During my time there, I spent one cold winter day working in freezing water up to my knees. That night my feet were swollen and white with frostbite. It didn't take me long after that to realize that finishing high school made more sense than a lifetime of manual labor. I returned to Alabama, but my damaged feet have been extremely sensitive to cold ever since.

There were even more reasons why I shouldn't hike the Trail.

I was forty-nine years old and had been a heavy smoker until two years earlier. It would be almost impossible to clear my calendar for a six-month trek. I didn't have enough money to finance that kind of venture. I don't like instant oatmeal, one of the main sources of sustenance on the Trail. I don't like to hike. Given a choice of recreational activities, hiking wouldn't even be on my list! I wasn't a serious backpacker with a lifelong yearning to walk the Appalachian Trail.

Besides all of this, I was blind. Getting around in town with Orient was one thing. Tramping through a forest with him was another. Orient was trained for city streets, not

mountain trails. No blind person had ever thru-hiked the
A.T. and I sure didn't feel ready to be the first.

Yet, I couldn't shake the growing impression that God
was calling me to do it.

I guess you could say it was a gradual revelation.

When Billy received a brochure describing Warren
Doyle's Appalachian Trail Institute to be held in December
'89, I decided to go — on the outside chance that things
really would work out for me to make the hike. I still wasn't
completely convinced it was the thing to do. But I found the
Institute encouraging, and while I was there I selected a
Trail name — something all thru-hikers do. It seemed
natural for us to be known as the Orient Express since the
first thing people usually ask me is "What's your dog's
name?"

That had a nice ring to it and made me feel like a real
thru-hiker, sitting there in a cozy lodge with a cup of tea!

Then, at a New Year's Eve service, the speaker
challenged us to seek God's will for the coming year and
be willing to do it. I told the Lord that if He wanted me to
hike the A.T., I was willing, but He would have to pave the
way for it. It didn't seem very likely that He would.

The first thing He'd have to do was clear my calendar
— for six months! On my refrigerator door at home, I keep
a series of notes to remind myself of upcoming
commitments. That's my version of an appointment calendar.
Between what I memorize and what I ask people to read for
me, it all stays pretty straight in my mind.

Early in January 1990, I realized the refrigerator door
had been empty for several weeks. My first reaction was,
"What did I do wrong that people stopped inviting me to
make speeches and conduct seminars?" Then I realized that
maybe *God* was at work. For the first time ever, my slate
was clean for almost the entire year. It became more
apparent that hiking the Trail was going to be a requirement,
not an option.

The clincher came when a friend, Gail Reams, asked me to speak for a meeting in April. I told her I probably couldn't do it because I might be hiking the Appalachian Trail. She got so excited she couldn't stop talking. She scheduled me to speak to her church in Greensboro and talk with several businessmen about the hike. Within a few weeks, people had donated money, equipment, and supplies.

I had passed the point of no return. At the very least, I felt obligated to get out on the Trail and get hurt "real bad" for them.

A dozen friends at church volunteered to help, and became the core of my support team in Burlington. They divided up the logistics of my life among them, and promised to do everything needed to keep me on the Trail.

"You keep walking," they said, "and we'll take care of the rest."

But hiking was only part of what I felt I had to do. If the purpose of being on the Trail was to talk to people about God and His love, I was definitely the wrong person for the job. I didn't know the first thing about what most people called "witnessing." I'd only been going to church for about two years. I certainly couldn't begin to argue theology or answer the hard questions that were sure to come. My lack of knowledge seemed to disqualify me faster than any of my physical shortcomings.

Finally, I decided that the talking would have to develop like the hiking. I couldn't plan it out or control it ahead of time. I had heard people talk about living by faith, and this was going to be my chance to discover what that was all about.

When I finally hit the Trail and people asked, "Why are you doing this?" I never knew how much to tell them. The easiest thing to say was that I was going because I felt God had called me to do it. But that didn't seem enough, since my purpose was to talk to people along the way and let them know what God had done in my life.

Most of the time, I ended up saying that I was hiking the Trail as a Christian witness mission. If they wanted to know more, I explained that my journey was a way of saying thanks to God for all the things He had done for me. I hoped that kind of openness wouldn't turn people off, because similar approaches had left *me* cold many times in the past. But I didn't know how else to say it and be completely honest. Rather than risk confusion, I just blurted it out.

I chose the third anniversary of my sobriety to start the hike. During the A.T. Institute, Warren Doyle had talked about the optimum time for hiking the Trail south to north. His suggestion was to leave from Georgia in March, because you have to be in Maine by the end of August or the first of September to avoid being stopped by the onset of winter. When I began thinking about a date to begin, I noticed on my calendar that March 8 was the anniversary of my sobriety. I couldn't imagine a better day to start. Somehow, it seemed fitting.

Chapter Seven

In the Limelight

The day after my encounter with dehydration and hypothermia in northern Georgia, Orient and I met up with photographer Tom Reed. We hiked together across a boulder field which the guidebook referred to as "5.8 of the roughest miles in Georgia." Tom took hundreds of pictures while Orient and I tried to navigate the jagged terrain. I must have fallen twenty times that day.

Exhausted, we pitched my tent before reaching the shelter, then talked into the night over cups of hot tea and a vast amount of macaroni and cheese, which I prepared. Tom had brought only candy bars and lunch meat, which he discovered wouldn't take him very far down the Trail.

He asked a lot of questions about my hike and what motivated me to attempt it. I answered as honestly as I could, trying to explain why I felt this was something God had called me to do. I asked him to be sure and highlight the spiritual dimension in his story. He said he would, and I could tell he meant it.

Without the spiritual aspect of my journey, I felt that I was just another guy heading north with his dog.

When the article appeared in the Atlanta paper, the spiritual part was missing. Tom later sent a note explaining that his story had been edited to fit space requirements. He apologized for any inaccuracies that may have resulted. I knew it wasn't Tom's fault, but it renewed my initial apprehension about being able to communicate the real reason behind this journey. I didn't have much recourse, so I just kept plodding along.

Hot Springs, North Carolina, a little mountain town of seven hundred people, was a welcome break from the Trail. According to one guidebook, the town had once been so popular as a health resort that seven passenger trains a day brought people from Atlanta to the warm baths. I was looking forward to a relaxing time in an out-of-the-way place where I could hide.

But soon after I arrived, on Good Friday, April 13, my uneasiness about publicity turned to genuine concern. Instead of being able to rest, do errands, and enjoy a day off, I spent several hours talking with newspaper reporters from nearby towns. It seemed that everyone asked the same questions and I was already getting tired of telling the same story. At the end of the day, I had still not done my laundry, purchased groceries or gotten a haircut.

That night, back at The Inn, I received a call from Atlanta. A producer of ABC's *World News Tonight* wanted to arrange an interview with me somewhere up the Trail. Whenever the phone rang after that, the other hikers joked that it was probably some other network anchorman wanting an interview.

There was a part of me that loved it. I've always enjoyed being the center of attention. A few years earlier, I would have called the newspapers and TV stations myself and tried to get all the publicity I could.

But this time it worried me. Being in the limelight could be the worst thing for me. I hoped to grow spiritually on the Trail, and publicity could interfere with that growth. I appreciated encouragement, but the last thing I needed was flattery.

I was also concerned that the press coverage might distort the meaning of the hike. I was on a Christian witness mission, pure and simple. I wasn't trying to strike a blow for persons with disabilities. I wasn't trying to prove that a person with enough willpower and determination could do anything he set his mind to do. I certainly wasn't trying to inspire people with handicaps to hike the A.T.

The more I thought about it, the more troubled I became. Would continuing requests for interviews take so much time that I wouldn't be able to complete the hike? Would other hikers see me as some kind of celebrity and avoid me on the Trail? Would people think I was doing this just to cash in on my notoriety after the hike? Did I have a responsibility to share my faith through the media as well as with individuals along the way?

After the phone quit ringing at The Inn and things quieted down, several of us hikers simultaneously suffered a "grease attack" — a craving for fried food. We headed for a local cafe and gorged ourselves on cheeseburgers, french fries, and chocolate shakes. Fortunately, the press wasn't there to document my incredible appetite.

Easter Sunday morning, I attended a sunrise service held by the Salvation Army at a little rural church. It was a wonderful time and filled my cup for the day. I was reminded that God was in charge of the hike, and everything was going to happen just the way He wanted it to.

I hit the Trail about 10:30 a.m., with the next cheeseburgers scheduled for Erwin, Tennessee, sixty-five miles away.

Along the way, I started meeting every night with some hikers I had met earlier on the Trail. Steve, a quiet, sensitive young man, whose Trail name was Talus, seemed fascinated with the way Orient and I were able to navigate. Sally, whose Trail name was Ms. Mainerd B — shortened from Maine or Bust — was a sweet, gutsy gal who had lost her right arm in an automobile accident a few years earlier. She shouldered her pack just like everyone else, and most people never noticed her prosthetic limb. Gary, an insulin-dependent diabetic, had been in the States for about six years, but still spoke with a crisp British accent. His diction and my drawl were about as far apart as you could get in the English language.

About this time things were leveling off. Orient was healing and feeling better daily, and I was losing a little weight. I was learning how to reduce the weight in my pack, and the going was easier physically.

Because of this, I did something I had never done before. Many people don't know that it's a bad idea to turn a Seeing Eye dog loose; a lot of people have lost their dogs that way. The dogs are wonderfully skilled at guiding, but they've never had any freedom.

Ever.

So they have no idea how to handle it. They're suddenly free, and they want to test the limits. So, the first thing they do is run off.

I knew all this better than most people, but because he'd done so well this far on the A.T., I wanted to give Orient some of the freedom he'd never had. I did it carefully; I didn't just turn him loose. I made sure people were watching him all the time. Since Orient had developed a strong attachment to Steve, I'd let him follow Steve when he'd go for water or take a bath at the end of the day. I always asked Steve to keep an eye on him to make sure he wouldn't run off. It worked perfectly.

Most of the time.

One afternoon, we set up an early camp at 3:00 p.m. It was like having a mini-day off, because the days were getting longer. We'd covered about fourteen miles that day and were all exhausted, even though there'd been no real incidents and the hiking was easy.

As I had done many times lately, I turned Orient loose. But this time, I didn't tell Steve. It had become such a regular thing with us, I just assumed he would watch out for Orient.

An hour or so later, when Steve came back, I said, "Come here, Orient."

Steve said, "Bill, Orient's not here."

I said, "Oh, yes he is. He followed you to get water."

But he hadn't.

About this time, another thru-hiker arrived from the Trail and said, "Are you guys talking about that big German Shepherd? Last time I saw him, he was running over that hill yonder, chasing a deer."

My heart sank. My whole body sank. "Without that dog," I cried, "I'm dead. I can't function. Besides, I love him!"

Other hikers were arriving now, and even though they'd been walking all day, they all went out in search of Orient, fanning out like spokes on a wheel.

Back at the camp, all kinds of thoughts were running through my mind. First, I could just see me telling the Seeing Eye that I'd turned my wonderful dog loose and he'd been killed by a car. I could see the accident. Then I began to think about him getting hurt, lying in the woods, crying in pain.

Then I got very angry. I thought, "Here I am, giving him a little extra freedom and he takes advantage of it and does this! He's got all of these tired people out searching for him while he's out having fun!" Boy, was I mad!

After a while, all the hikers returned. Nobody had seen any evidence of Orient or the deer.

Steve was the last to return. When he told me he hadn't seen anything, I said we needed to hike out of there to the Forest Service and ask them to help us. Maybe they could even get a helicopter.

It was about 5:00 p.m. by then. As we started our hike to the nearest road, which was about three miles away — we didn't know exactly where — I asked the guy who had seen Orient and the deer which hill he had seen them on. After he told us, I asked Steve to lead me to the top of that hill. Yelling "Orient!" over and over as loudly as I could, I turned in different directions.

Between crying and yelling and thinking I'd killed the best dog that had ever lived, I was a wreck. Then, all of a sudden, Orient scampered up! I could tell by his behavior he knew something was up. He was like a bad boy who has been testing the waters; but he came.

I had to praise him, because the worst thing you can do to a dog is to severely reprimand him when he's just done something right. Orient's last memory was of obeying me — he didn't remember the running away. I had to praise him for returning or he wouldn't return the next time.

Meanwhile, I was having mixed emotions. One part of me wanted to punish him, but another part of me was so glad he was back and the pressure was off, that all I could do was roll around on the ground, loving him.

Then I stood up and sternly told him, "You're grounded until Katahdin." Steve roared with laughter.

From then on, except for brief intervals, I kept Orient attached to the leash. Even when we slept, I hooked him to the zipper of my sleeping bag. The only other time he was ever off the leash was in a cabin in Connecticut — and that had disastrous results also!

When I ambled into Erwin five days later (with Orient firmly under leash!), an ABC crew from Atlanta was waiting to meet me and get to work. Kent Garland, a local resident and long-time friend of hikers, took me to the grocery store and the laundromat as the TV crew recorded it all. That afternoon, I set up my tent along the Nolichucky River. This would serve as a backdrop for the interview with correspondent Al Dale.

A number of newspaper reporters were waiting for interviews as well, and the press activities continued into the night. Several other thru-hikers and I were at a hostel at the Nolichucky Expedition Center, and I didn't want the interviews to dominate their evening. But by 11:00 p.m., I still hadn't had lunch, much less supper. So I told the reporters that my next interview would be with someone holding a pizza in his hand, not only for me, but for the other thru-hikers — who had also been answering questions. That produced a flurry of activity and, more importantly, some food and cold sodas for everyone. I didn't want to be impolite, but I didn't see any point in starving either.

The next morning, the ABC crew asked me to hike one section of the Trail several times so they could shoot it from different angles. That didn't make any sense at all to a thru-hiker. I began to realize how much time and energy went into producing something that wouldn't last more than three minutes on TV. I appreciated their kindness and interest, but wondered how I could accommodate everyone and still make it to Mt. Katahdin.

Four days later, a helicopter bearing a news crew from WRAL-TV in Raleigh, North Carolina, was waiting on the ground when Orient and I emerged into a clearing. Reporter Leslie Boney rushed up to meet us and arrange an interview at a road crossing up ahead. That day I was again accompanied by Steve, Sally, Gary, and by another hiker, Al Sanborn. Orient and I led the way to the road crossing at a brisk clip while the others followed. I could hear a lot of voices near the Trail, so I asked one man what they were doing there. He told me that most of them had never had a close look at a helicopter — or at a blind man with a dog hiking the Appalachian Trail.

"Have you seen that blind man?" he asked.

I chuckled, quickened my pace through the crowd, and called back, "He's about four hundred yards behind me."

The interview took the rest of the afternoon, but was followed by a cookout for all the hikers, hosted by a family from Johnson City. After seeing an article about the Orient Express in their local newspaper, they had come out to say hello and offer their encouragement. We gratefully accepted their handshakes — and their hamburgers!

The next morning, another helicopter flew in with a TV crew from Bristol, Tennessee. They landed near our campsite and asked if they could wire me for sound and follow us along the Trail for a mile or so. Orient smiled at the cameramen, cocked his head and pricked his ears, so they forgot about me for a while. But not long enough!

My granddaddy used to call this kind of situation "plus one, minus two." That pretty well described my feelings about meeting the press at every turn. They were wonderful people and very gracious, but they had a time-consuming job to do. My task was getting to Maine, and I wasn't sure we could both accomplish our goals.

When Al Dale's story aired on ABC's *World News Tonight* in May, and an article about Orient and me appeared in *USA Today*, my low-profile days on the Trail were over. People began talking about how many millions would see the Orient Express on television and in newspapers.

I tried not to play the numbers game in my mind, because if I did, it was hard to keep it all in perspective.

Occasionally, the reporters would ask about my life before the hike began. Was I married? Did I have children? Did I have a job? Had I always been religious? I didn't have anything to hide, but at the same time, I wasn't sure they wanted the whole story. That seemed better suited to private conversations.

And by this time, I was discovering another reason for the hike. I found myself dealing for the first time with the loss of my parents. I had been anesthetized by alcohol when first my mother and then my father died. I had tried to bury the pain of our earlier conflicts and misunderstanding in a dark corner of my heart.

Each day and night on the Trail, with a clear mind and time to think, allowed long-forgotten memories to rise to the surface. I hadn't set out to do this as some sort of quest for healing, but that healing was happening.

The Orient Express in 'civilian' clothes, a week before beginning their trek on the A.T.
"I didn't see any reason why we couldn't make twenty miles a day."
Credit: Jack Sink, Burlington Times-News

A narrow ledge and steep drop near Hot Springs, NC., required full concentration.
"Orient knew how far down it was and he kept us on the Trail."
Credit: Larry Hoffman, The Asheville Citizen

Kent Garland of Erwin, TN, completes Bill's personal check for groceries. "Hundreds of people all along the Trail went out of their way to give me a hand." *Credit: Keith Whitson, The Erwin Record*

ABC's Al Dale launched Bill into the national television spotlight on *World News Tonight*. "That was the end of my low profile days on the Trail."
Credit: Charles Edwards, The Erwin Record

Bill and Orient learned to navigate the Trail in the rugged mountains of Georgia. "Steep descents were treacherous for me. No one ever got killed falling uphill."
Credit: Tom Reed, Stock South

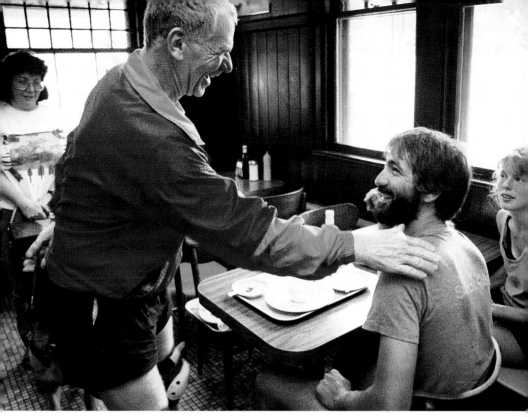

Anna Vail (left) and Bill greet thru-hikers Rick and Shirley Alexander (The Total Recs) at a Trail-side cafe. "Trail friends became family as our paths crossed time after time."
Credit: Gary O'Brien, The Charlotte Observer

Bill tells a day-hiker how to locate a Trail crossing along New York Highway 17. "Years ago I decided to do everything I could not to <u>act</u> blind."
Credit: Gary O'Brien, The Charlotte Observer

Orient learned to lead Bill to the carved wooden signs along the Trail. "Hiking alone, I craved information about location and distance more than anything."
Credit: Tom Reed, Stock South

Drying out at Muskrat Creek, NC, the only A-frame shelter on the A.T. "A thru-hiker axiom we soon learned was 'No rain, no Maine.'" *Credit: John Carter*

"I often wondered about the man who called this a footpath." *Credit: David McCasland*

"I wasn't mentally or physically prepared for the endless array of rocks." *Credit: Bill Greene, Boston Globe*

A broken rib, bloody knees, and bruised arms resulted from thousands of falls. "Every time I went down, I tried to be thankful I wasn't hurt worse than I was."
Credit: Bill Greene, Boston Globe

September 26. Mt. Madison, NH. Bill hiked 7 1/2 hours and covered only 3 miles. "One of the longest days of my life." *Credit: Bill Greene, Boston Globe*

Peter Martel (Mr. Moleskin) offers a steadying hand on an icy log bridge over Katahdin Stream. "I told Warren Doyle I'd crawl to Maine if I had to." *Credit: Bill Greene, Boston Globe*

Chapter Eight

Family Week

After my parents died, my life still had one major theme — alcohol. This had been the theme of my whole adult life. As far back as 1961, I had almost killed myself with the booze I used to deaden the pain I felt.

On Christmas Eve of that year, I was lying in a Mississippi hospital in the advanced stages of alcohol-induced hepatitis. My father came to visit me, and I overheard the doctor tell him that, without a miracle, I wouldn't live through the night. I closed my eyes, thinking how nice it would be to go to sleep and not have to wake up in the morning.

I was twenty-one years old.

When I did awake the next day, I was markedly better, but I never considered the change miraculous. A few months after my recovery, I was drinking just as heavily as before. It took another twenty-five years before I was ready to admit that I had a problem with alcohol.

I had become an alcoholic on August 16, 1940 — the day I was born.

Alcoholism seemed to come with the territory in my extended family. During a boyhood visit to my grandfather's farm, he once told me, "Irwins can't drink." I should have been able to look around at my relatives and see what he meant, but it was years before I understood.

My family was one of the wealthiest in our town, and I never lacked for anything. Both my mother and father had grown up poor and were determined that their kids would never be touched by poverty. My parents were good people, wonderful in many ways, but there wasn't a lot of affection and encouragement in our home. Some of the ways my father punished me were even abusive, physically and emotionally. Instead of being able to deal with this, I just passed the insults and criticism on to others.

After running away at fifteen and working in the Texas oil fields, I had returned to school. When I took my first drink the night of high-school graduation, it turned out to be a whole bottle. That evening, the more I drank, the more wonderful I became in my own eyes. It was an inner blindness that would persist long after my physical sight was gone.

All through my years as a chemist, school teacher, and laboratory owner, my alcoholism had persisted. By 1987, my addiction to alcohol, along with other obsessive-compulsive behaviors had taken me through four failed marriages and a host of other broken relationships. My adult children were struggling with many of the same self-indulgent habits they had grown up seeing in me.

On February 13 that year, my twenty-three-year-old son, Jeff, called from Birmingham, Alabama. He was crying as he told me that, if he didn't break his cocaine habit, he was going to die.

"Dad, will you help me?" he asked.

It was the first time in his life he had ever asked for my help and I couldn't say no, even though our relationship had always been stormy. I talked with several people and we arranged for Jeff to be admitted to a treatment center in Birmingham.

Three days after Jeff's call, I took my first Seeing Eye dog, Jorie, to a vet. Although Jorie had been retired a few months earlier because of hip dysplasia and I had already received my second dog, Sailor, Jorie still lived with me.

Jorie's condition had worsened and he could no longer stand by himself. He was almost eleven years old and the vet said it was cruel to let him go on that way.

"He's in a lot of pain," he told me. "The kindest thing would be to put him to sleep. You might want to think about it for a few days."

Put Jorie to sleep? He had served me faithfully and loved me for nine years and I couldn't think about life without him. He had given me independence and helped me out of the bottomless pit of depression.

But I knew it wasn't right to prolong his suffering. I told the vet that if I left with Jorie, I'd never be able to bring him back.

"Don't tell me when you're going to put him to sleep," I said. "Have him cremated and give me the ashes."

I asked if I could have a little time alone with Jorie, and the vet left the room. I sat down on the floor beside him, rubbed his head and told him what a good boy he was. I talked to him for a few minutes about where we'd gone and what we'd done. I told him how much I loved him. Then I left.

A few days later, he was gone.

The Friday after Jorie died, I sent a friend to the liquor store for a supply that should have lasted me two weeks. By Sunday morning, it was all gone. But I had not experienced any relief or high. I was shaking and afraid, too drunk to walk across my living room, yet my mind had not been numbed. I was still reeling from my crushing sense of loss.

Alcohol had tricked and embarrassed me many times before, but this was the first time it had failed me.

Shortly after Jeff checked into the treatment center, one of the counselors called, asking me to come for what they called "Family Week." I told her I'd be happy to come and asked, "What time is happy hour?" She didn't laugh.

The sober reality was that I had to spend a week in the treatment center interacting with Jeff, his mother, and the staff. I wasn't anxious to do it, but agreed because it seemed necessary for Jeff's recovery.

Long before I arrived, the treatment center staff had the lowdown on me. They carefully watched me unpack my suitcase to make sure I didn't have a bottle inside, then told me that for the next seven days, I couldn't smoke in the building or drink any alcohol. In addition, the only coffee I would be served was decaffeinated.

I immediately began planning my escape!

Despite the pain, it turned out to be the most significant week of my life. For the first time, I had to listen to Jeff say what he felt about himself, his mother, his brother and sister, and me. My attitude had always been, "I don't want to hear it," and his feelings had stayed locked up inside, except when we had a shouting match.

Now I knew I needed to listen to Jeff, but I wasn't about to accept what the treatment center staff was telling me about myself. Early on, it had become apparent that they were trying to make me admit I had a problem with alcohol. I let them know very clearly that I was there to help my son, and my behavior was none of their business. I was a well-respected consultant in the area of legal toxicology and I had forgotten more about addiction than they had ever known.

I harassed the staff unmercifully and defied their every attempt to convince me that my life was out of control. When they asked if I ever drank in the morning or had times I couldn't remember, I lied and said no. I knew all the right answers, but my life *had* become completely unmanageable. Things were definitely out of control; and I had no idea how to change that.

Inside, I felt crushed under the weight of circumstances that became more overwhelming every day. A few months earlier, I had left my job after the boss and I reached a mutual understanding — I could either quit or he would fire me. Just before this, I had lost my life savings in a foolish business venture.

My father had died the preceding November, after a long battle with bone cancer. Losing him made me realize I had never dealt with my mother's lingering illness and death seven years before. With him gone, I now felt stripped of human love. Perhaps to compensate, I had become addicted to a woman in New Jersey, and that relationship took ninety percent of my emotional energy and nearly all my money.

There wasn't enough room on a 747 jet for all my emotional baggage.

After a few days in the treatment center, I couldn't sleep at night. God seemed to be confronting me with who I was, and I didn't like what I saw. Events from my life that had been swept under the rug of conscious memory now became vividly clear in my mind. It was like watching a videotape of every person I had hurt or wronged. Without the anesthetic of alcohol, I had no way to stop the pain.

As I struggled to face myself, one voice said: "Listen, if we can just make it for two more days, we can get out of here, stop at the liquor store, get us a bottle of Jim Beam, go back to North Carolina and never have to worry with this garbage again."

But there was another voice saying, "If you don't admit you're an alcoholic while you're here, you never will."

Even though the treatment center staff stopped trying to confront me, the pressure inside me increased. I don't think I slept for the rest of the week.

When graduation day rolled around, every patient received a key chain signifying completion of the program, and each accompanying family member was called on to say a brief word in reply. Jeff got his key chain, and my dog, Sailor, got a little bag of dog biscuits. I was wondering what to say when they called on me. I decided to use my standard quip and say, "My name's Bill, I used to work for the company that makes Valium, and I love to drink."

But when they called my name, I stood up and said, "My name's Bill and... and I'm an alcoholic."

The audience, including my family, was stunned. My first reaction was to wonder where the ventriloquist was, because surely I hadn't said those words. But now I believe there was a divine intervention in my life... and that was the beginning of my spiritual awakening.

The next evening I was back in Burlington, feeling very strange without a drink in my hand. I had no desire for alcohol. My need for alcohol had been miraculously taken away. But I didn't know what to do with myself. So I asked my daughter, Marianne, if she'd take me to the local meeting of a twelve-step program for recovering alcoholics. The people at the treatment center had urged me to get involved in this. I wasn't convinced I needed it, but I decided it wouldn't hurt to try.

After the first meeting, I resolved not to go back. They just weren't my kind of people. They were blue-collar, and I was a professional. They were unpolished, and I was used to moving in a more sophisticated crowd. They were drunks; I was an alcoholic. Maybe there was another group somewhere with people who were more like me.

A couple of days later, I telephoned the treatment center to see if they knew of a different group around Burlington. The staff woman was sympathetic and told me she knew just how I felt. "You do need a more sophisticated group," she said, and promised to put me in touch with a man who could help me find it. In the meantime, she asked me to keep attending this group for a couple of weeks until things fell into place. Just to make her happy, I agreed.

One night at a meeting, a man in our group said this was the only place where a plumber could teach a priest how to live. That intrigued me and brought me back to the next meeting, where a fellow gave the best advice I'd ever heard about living one day at a time.

"When you go to bed at night," he said, "kick your shoes so far back under the bed that you have to get down on your knees the next morning to get them. While you're down there, ask God to help you make it through the day. That night, thank Him for what He did for you and kick your shoes way back under the bed again."

Two weeks turned into ten, and the lady from the treatment center never called back. By then, I had learned what she knew all along. I didn't need a new group, just a new perspective on who I was and what kind of help I needed.

Two months after acknowledging my alcoholism, I was teaching a toxicology seminar in Florida. I dismissed the morning session early, and headed downstairs because I was out of cigarettes. I was standing in line at the hotel gift shop when the thought came to me, "You aren't going to smoke anymore." It wasn't a voice or a vision, just a matter-of-fact thought that was almost like an announcement.

When I reached the counter and the woman asked what I wanted, I told her I couldn't remember, and left the shop. After smoking as many as five packs of cigarettes every day for thirty-nine years, my desire for tobacco was gone.

I began wondering which one of my addictions God was going to put His finger on next.

I hadn't struggled to break the chains of alcohol addiction. I can't tell you why God took it so quickly and completely from me while others struggle with it for years. I guess He knew my weaknesses and dealt with me accordingly. But while that desire was gone, all the destructive patterns of thought and behavior were still in place.

I was basically a manipulator who used other people to get what I wanted. When they refused to fit in with my plans, I was ready to discard them. I had used alcohol to deaden the pain of emotional losses and submerge the things I didn't want to think about. Now, with a clear mind, I wanted to face the issues and deal with the causes of my problems, not just the effects.

Step Four in the twelve-step program of recovery basically brought me face-to-face with these issues. It involves making "a searching and fearless moral inventory of ourselves."

That painful process generated a long list of people and events I had tried to ignore. I had been a great blamer, accusing my family, friends, and associates for causing everything that was wrong in my life. Now, each week, with the support of the people in my group, I was able to assume more responsibility for the failures that were mine alone.

Steps Eight and Nine involve listing all the persons I had harmed, and making direct amends wherever possible without hurting others. That was tough. I began with face-to-face apologies, and found that each one removed a little more of my burden of guilt. I made telephone calls and wrote letters to try and reach everyone who appeared on my list.

I was determined to work the twelve steps, one at a time, because I was discovering how good it felt to be at peace, sober, and alive. When people asked me to explain what had happened, I couldn't find the words because I didn't fully understand it myself.

I became more aware of the world around me, a world I had been deadened to for so long. My own yard became a different place, alive with sounds and smells I hadn't noticed in years. I was struck with the amazing complexity of God's creation and the simple beauty of it all.

For me, seeing God in the created world was a big part of working on Step Eleven — seeking through prayer and meditation to improve my conscious contact with God, praying to know His will and finding the power to carry it out. But when I tried doing this, I could never seem to get very far.

Then, in September of 1988, I spent a weekend at Vade Mecum, a beautiful retreat center in the Great Smoky Mountains of western North Carolina. One afternoon, a friend I greatly respected asked me a question. "Bill," he said, "what's your relationship with Jesus Christ?"

That kind of question was usually enough to send me out the door, but that day, I gave him an honest answer and said, "I don't have one, but I'd like to know more about it."

We walked up to a little open air chapel on the mountainside and he explained what it meant to commit my life completely to Christ. He read something called The Sinner's Prayer and I repeated the words aloud after him. I told God I was sorry for all the wrong things I had done and the person I had been, and asked Him to forgive me. I opened the door of my life to Jesus Christ and asked Him to come in, take over as manager and run things His way. After I finished, Bill gave me the biggest bear hug I'd ever had.

"Bill, you're a new man in Christ," he told me. "And things are going to be different in your life from now on." I hoped so, but wondered how he could be so sure.

It was clear God was up to something in my life, but I had no idea where it was all headed. Soon, I realized that I needed to stop trying to control the people in my life, particularly my adult children. I began trying to listen to them more and advise them less — to let them take the course they felt was best, instead of insisting that they go my way.

You'd have to talk to my children and the people around me during that first year to get an objective opinion about the changes in my life. Some were obvious and others were more subtle, but all of them were amazing to me. Inside, I could feel the anger and bitterness begin to subside. It was as if someone had turned off the burner under a tea kettle.

All I knew was that I had cracked the door of my life open to God and He had gone to work in as many ways as I would let Him.

I was more surprised than anyone at the results.

Chapter Nine

Through Other Eyes

Here I was, eighteen months later, still surprised at the results.

For most hikers, the rewards of the Appalachian Trail were primarily visual. After struggling up a mountain all morning, they would often stop for an hour to drink in the panoramic view of the surrounding peaks and valleys. People often wondered what rewards were in the hike for me, since I couldn't see any of that.

"Do you feel cheated," they asked, "because of all the beauty you can't see?"

When Helen Keller was asked, "Can you see a world?" she replied, "I can see, and that is why I can be happy, in what you call the dark, but which to me is golden. I can see a God-made world, not a man-made world."

There were times when I wished I *could* see the colors and the vistas other hikers described to me. But I was learning, like Helen Keller, to experience nature in beautiful and exciting new ways. As Orient and I hiked the Trail day after day, usually alone, the world around us was a constant source of wonder and pleasure.

Often, I was aware of a person or object near me, even though I couldn't see them. The combination of sound, skin sensitivity, and smell produces a kind of sixth sense known as "facial perception," which I relied on heavily. Along the

Trail, I could tell if I was walking under low-hanging branches or among tall trees. My perception of a large rock face on one side was different from my sense of the empty space below a narrow ledge. I could feel the vastness of a high mountain and the depth of a wooded valley. Facial perception was the reason I sometimes extended my arm toward a tree or rock that I couldn't see, but knew was there.

Sighted hikers do experience visual rewards that were hidden from me on the A.T. But there are things that none of us can see unless we look through the eyes of our souls. For me, those images were like time exposures created as each succeeding day and night allowed a small portion of light to leave its mark on the film of my mind.

I guess a lot of what I "saw" came through my other senses. I loved the sound of the wind blowing through the forest. It sounded different in the early spring in Georgia, North Carolina, and Tennessee than it did in the summer, when the vegetation was lush and thick. The breeze told me whether I was surrounded by deciduous trees or a pine forest. It rustled leaves, but it whistled through evergreen needles. Sometimes, the creaking of a tree sounded like someone talking or the groaning of timbers on an old ship at sea.

On bald mountain tops, the wind often became a force that I felt more than heard. More than once, Orient and I had to drop down flat to keep from being blown over by a blast of air on its way from one part of God's world to another.

By the time we crossed the state line into Virginia, it was early May, and the air was filled with the unmistakable scents of hundreds of different flowers, plants, and trees. The rhododendron were magnificent, along with the mountain laurel and the azaleas.

Orient seemed to be enjoying himself more as we got to Virginia. In the city, he was required to ignore his keen sense of smell and concentrate on what he saw and heard. Out here, he was able to let his nose slip back in gear and tune in to everything around him.

That's something else I discovered: I was becoming attuned to Orient's moods. His feelings had been among my biggest concerns from the very beginning. When Orient had those sores after the first few days of hiking and I had had to assume his pack weight, I knew if anything happened to Orient I would have to stop.

But I had to be tuned in to his psyche as well as his physical condition. And now, after about five hundred miles, I could finally tell when things were more than he could handle.

A dog is a sprinter, not an endurance animal. It dawned on me in the early summer heat of Virginia that it was going to take Orient a long time to develop the kind of stamina necessary for this adventure. Whenever Orient got tired, we took a break in the shade until he was ready to go again.

(One of the interesting things was that, in the days ahead, as I gradually got weaker, Orient got stronger. By the time we got to New Hampshire, he was charged up and ready to go all the time — and I could barely stagger along.)

I had something in common with Orient by the time we got to the Virginia state line. I was surprised at how my own sense of smell seemed to become more acute the longer I was on the Trail. When it was about to rain, I usually caught the smell long before the clouds covered the sun and the thunder began to roll.

Often, I noticed the faint aroma of wood smoke a mile or more before I reached a shelter in the evening. One afternoon I passed a young couple just out for the day, and I was stopped in my tracks by the fragrance of the girl's perfume. After weeks with a bunch of sweaty thru-hikers and one sweaty dog, I couldn't believe *anyone* could smell that good! The couple kept on walking, but I stayed there for a while enjoying the lingering traces of perfume in the air.

I also came to appreciate silence. It was one of the most stunning experiences on the Trail. Sometimes when I paused to catch my breath, the complete absence of any sound was overpowering. It completely captured my attention. Had I ever heard total silence before? No, not that I could remember. And where else in today's world could I find a few seconds void of any sound? The moments without a bird singing, a twig snapping or other sounds were rare, but I began to listen for them and to savor the stillness for as long as it lasted.

Within a short time, certain familiar sounds developed new meaning. I had always enjoyed listening to running water, but had never associated it with survival. On a day when the temperature was near ninety degrees and the humidity about ninety percent, there was nothing to compare with the gurgling of a brook as its cold, life-giving water crossed the Trail.

This was the first time in my life that I couldn't turn a tap, drink from a fountain, or walk to a vending machine any time I wanted a cold drink. I usually left camp each morning carrying two quarts of water, but it rarely lasted until noon. Locating water was a problem for sighted hikers; it was doubly difficult for me. My cassette tape guide told me where good water was supposed to be, but finding enough to satisfy my thirst was something I never again took for granted after the first few days in Georgia.

Sometimes the nearest water would be two-tenths of a mile off the A.T. This was a major concern for me until I learned that, if you turn a thirsty dog loose, he'll find water. A dog's keen sense of smell and hearing will lead him right to it. Orient could hear water minutes before I knew it was close by.

Another thing I learned about water was that, no matter where I was on a mountain, there would be water at the bottom. If you went low enough on the mountain, you'd always find water. There'd always be a spring or a stream somewhere if you could just wait.

But even if you found water, there was a problem. Some of the streams were infected with giardia, a microscopic organism present in surface water supplies all along the Trail. Even a clear, cold, flowing stream could be contaminated with it. Unless water came from a spring, most hikers treated it with iodine tablets, pumped it through a portable filter, or boiled it when they made camp.

Giardia was the curse and dread of thru-hikers. Symptoms of the disease include diarrhea, abdominal cramps, and vomiting. The only way to overcome it was to get off the Trail, see a doctor, and obtain prescription medicine.

Orient couldn't detect giardia, but he had a pretty good nose for water. Sometimes he would lead me off the Trail to a brook or spring no one else knew was there! If he wouldn't drink from it, I bypassed it, too. No matter how thirsty we were, there were several streams Orient would simply refuse to go close to. In time, I came to trust him. I would not collect water he wouldn't drink. And I didn't get giardia.

Once, we came upon a group of people who were talking around a spring and drinking the water. Orient walked up, sniffed it, but wouldn't drink it. When the people invited me to have some, I said we'd pass. When they asked why, I said it was because my dog wouldn't drink it and dogs are smarter than people! I laughed when I said it, and they laughed too — but we still waited until the next source to drink.

I also gained a new appreciation for the simple privilege of protection from the elements. Under a tin-roofed shelter or inside a nylon tent, I could enjoy the sound of pounding rain. On the Trail, it could only be endured.

My excitement in discovering this new world was somewhat tempered by realizing how much my blindness hindered me. In the normal course of city life, I had come to consider blindness a minor inconvenience. Sometimes it could even provide a slight advantage in making a positive impression. But on the Trail, I found out that being without sight was a terrific disadvantage.

One of my greatest difficulties in hiking alone was uncertainty, especially about where I was or how far I had to go. In the mountains, sounds could be very deceptive. One afternoon I quickened my pace after hearing the sound of traffic on a highway. The prospect of finding a country store and a cold soda at the road crossing spurred me on. But it was two hours before I covered the distance to the road. The cars that sounded so close had been nearly four miles away.

Naturally, a daily concern for a blind hiker is just staying on the A.T. The blazes offered reassurance to sighted hikers every few hundred feet, but Orient and I had to work together to decide which way to go as we crossed logging roads, streams and other trails. New Trail relocations always threw me off.

Some days, I felt Orient was following the scent of other hikers. On the long stretches when no one could take showers, I could almost follow the smell myself! That was fine as long as our hiking friends stayed on the A.T. Many times when we became confused, I stopped and just asked the Lord to show us which way to go.

When we didn't encounter other hikers, the information I craved more than anything else concerned distance. How far had I come? How far was the next road crossing or shelter?

Hikers were not always an accurate source of information. It seemed they always told me that things were closer than they actually were.

"The next shelter? Three-eighths of a mile ahead. You'll be there in ten minutes."

Half an hour later, I'd still be walking, with no sign of a shelter. No matter what I was looking for, people seemed to tell me it was only three-eighths of a mile.

The occasional carved or routed wooden signs were a great help but were often far apart. Orient soon learned to stop next to each one so I could read it with my fingers. The signs were official, but I frequently questioned them, too.

"Surely we've come more than 2.6 miles," I would say aloud, even if Orient was the only one with me. If a sign said the next shelter was six-tenths of a mile, a hundred yards later, I would be convinced we had passed the shelter.

I found myself relying more and more on the sun for direction. Hiking in bright sunshine, I rarely got disoriented. But on cloudy days, disorientation was a problem. I used the sun to determine north or south, so its presence was critical for me.

Each evening, before I settled in, I would tie a bandana on the tent peg or make a knot in something that would help me point my head towards the north when I got in bed. That way, I would know which direction to head when I got up. (The Trail is rarely marked north or south, but it only occasionally departs from that orientation during the course of a day.)

Thru-hikers on the Trail usually got a big kick out of the questions asked by people out for a short hike.

"Y'all hiking the Trail?" they'd ask. "Seen any snakes?" or "Seen any bears?"

One of my favorite replies was, "I haven't seen a snake in twenty years." It was true. Of course, I hadn't seen anything else in that long, either!

Other things that people did were also humorous. When talking with me, some people went out of their way to avoid the word "see." They'd stammer a little, then ask about what I had heard or encountered.

I never made those distinctions when I described what I had "seen."

After hearing the chattering of a squirrel or the crashing of a deer bounding away from a nearby thicket, I felt I had seen the animals themselves. Thirty years of sight had given me a memory bank full of images. Then, too, sound and smell frequently combined to let me know what animals were nearby. Grouse and wild turkeys were easy to identify. Porcupines were more difficult. Skunks were a cinch.

Usually, Orient would alert me to the presence of an animal long before I knew it was there. I could tell immediately if Orient raised his head, pricked his ears, or began looking for something he had smelled or heard.

When it came to priority of senses, Orient got his information from his nose first, his ears second, and his eyes last. Milo Pearsall, who trains dogs for search and rescue, described the difference in human and canine scent this way:

"One of the substances released by human perspiration is butyric acid. If one gram (a small drop in the bottom of a teaspoon) were to be spread throughout a ten-story building, a person could smell it at the window only at the moment of release. If this same amount were spread over the entire city of Philadelphia, a dog could smell it anywhere, even up to an altitude of three hundred feet."[1]

That gave me a lot more respect for Orient's willingness to sleep with me in the tent, especially when it was a long time between showers!

But Orient didn't usually pay much attention to animals, because he had been trained to ignore them. A squirrel or rabbit or snake could cross two feet in front of him and he would never miss a step. So when he came to a complete stop one day on a narrow portion of the Trail, I thought we had met a hiker coming from the other direction.

---

[1] Scent: Training to Track, Search, and Rescue, by Milo D. Pearsall and Hugo Verbruggen, M.D. Alpine Publications, Inc., Loveland, CO, 1982, p5.

I said hello and wondered why the person didn't say anything in reply.

I don't remember what I said next, probably something about the weather or a question about the Trail, but Orient growled and I became aware that whatever was standing ahead of us was grinding its teeth.

It was either a very tense, very hungry thru-hiker — or a bear.

There are so many bears in the Smokies that the shelters are enclosed by chain-link fences and it is illegal to camp outside them. On the Trail, bears have a reputation for boldness in confronting hikers. Their usual approach is to intimidate a hiker into dropping his pack and running away. That leaves the bear free to enjoy the granola bars or a candy bar or two.

It also leaves the hiker free to cover a portion of the Trail faster than he or she had ever thought possible.

Back at Neels Gap, a ranger had told me that the best way to face a bear was to stand your ground and talk to it in a quiet voice, just as you would a person. When I realized that the thing on the Trail in front of me was a bear, I tried to explain that my food bag was almost empty and that I hadn't seen a candy bar in days. I mentioned that I was just passing through the area and promised not to pick any of the berries it might be interested in. I went on to explain that my furry friend beside me was not a little bear, but a dog that I really needed if I was going to get on down the Trail and out of the way.

We must have carried on a one-sided conversation for about five minutes, with me giving continual assurances that I was harmless and the bear steadily grinding its teeth. Finally, it turned around and ambled back down the Trail before crashing off into the woods.

Stories about hikers being attacked by bears on the A.T. are numerous, but actual cases are few. The most frequent results of bear encounters are shredded packs carried by hikers who have been scared to death. I was glad I had met my bear so I could tell the story, but I wasn't at all interested in its happening again.

Orient seemed relieved as well. People often asked me what he would do if I were attacked by an animal or a person. It's hard to say, because Seeing Eye dogs are bred for an easy-going temperament and taught to be non-aggressive. Nothing in his training or experience would lead him to believe he was supposed to protect me from physical harm. In a threatening situation, *I* was the one who was supposed to protect *him*. Still, if I were attacked or injured, maybe he'd at least be willing to go for help. But knowing Orient as I do, I think he'd probably just wag his tail and lick the bad guy's hand.

Besides encounters with bears, steep descents of any kind were very difficult for me. They seemed to take forever. My standard question was, "How far below sea level is the next shelter?" Only the uninitiated hikers tried to answer it by giving me the exact elevation.

"It *must* be below sea level," I would tell them, "because we've already come down about twenty thousand feet from the top of the last mountain." It wasn't really my brain that made the exaggerations. The message came directly from my feet.

Despite my aching feet, my sense of wonder continued to grow. I had probably been in the fourth grade when I learned that the rain falls in the mountains, the water runs to the sea, the evaporation forms clouds and the whole thing starts over. On the Trail, I saw it with my soul for the first time. This new understanding didn't happen in a week or even a month. But gradually, I became more aware of a God-made world, working according to His design.

It was not an intellectual awareness. It was spiritual. For me, it was the difference between drawing the molecular structure of water and drinking from a spring. My fellow hikers discovered it by watching the sunset, not the lights of Manhattan. It happened on a footpath, not a freeway.

Maybe that was part of what drove Benton MacKaye, Myron Avery and their successors to establish the A.T. and fight to see it stretch unbroken from Maine to Georgia. Early in the twentieth century, they began their efforts to create a pathway through the wilderness and to preserve it for the generations to come. At a time when people were migrating from farms to assembly line jobs in sprawling cities, they created a place to which others could escape. The length of the Trail was undoubtedly an effort to make it accessible to the greatest number of people possible.

For some reason, I had thought the Trail would have been laid out with some sympathy for the hiker. Instead, it seemed that the designers delighted in winding it over every available peak, through every precipitous canyon, and across every jagged boulder field. Even Orient would, at times, try to find an easier path than the one marked as the A.T. But in the final analysis, the difficulty and physical challenge of the Trail probably beckoned as many hikers as did the beauty.

Henry David Thoreau's unsuccessful attempt to climb Katahdin back in 1846 undoubtedly lured many later readers of his works to the untamed wilderness he described. Without benefit of the Trail, he and his Penobscot Indian guides had ascended into the clouds, stopping short of what they thought was the highest peak.

Earl Shaffer completed what is generally accepted as the first continuous end-to-end hike over the A.T. in 1948. His thru-hike became the inspiration for thousands of others who set out to walk the distance — and be changed by the experience.

Some hike the Trail for only a day and find themselves renewed. But continuous weeks in the God-made world can yield a fortune of insight. The Lord must have known it would take a long journey to show me all I needed to see.

Chapter Ten

Family Matters

It didn't take long on the Trail for me to discover that thru-hikers made up a unique family — and I was definitely part of it. Most of us had little in common except the Trail, but that was enough to bind us together.

In almost any other situation, our ages, occupations, and backgrounds would have kept us apart. On the A.T., none of that mattered and we rarely discussed it. We were hiking in the same rain, shivering in the same cold, basking in the same sunshine, and striving to reach the same goal. Being on the Trail made us hikers. Being together made us a family.

I had first met Steve, Sally, and Gary in Hot Springs, North Carolina. We stayed at the same hostel and enjoyed a couple of enormous meals together at a local cafe. They ribbed me about becoming a media celebrity, and I told them they needed a mature person to chaperone them along the Trail. We had a lot of fun and ended up shelter-hopping together for the better part of three weeks.

Sally and Gary were with me the day I stopped for lunch at a little trail-side store and snack bar. After we ordered, the owner told me that, as soon as I got my food, Orient and I would have to step outside. "We don't allow dogs in here," she said.

I said, "Ma'am, it's all right for us to stay inside, since Orient is a Seeing Eye dog. He's allowed to be in restaurants."

When she insisted that we eat outside, I reaffirmed my intention to stay.

"That dog stinks," she said. "We have regular customers who eat in here and we aren't about to drive them away."

I knew that Orient didn't smell as if he'd just emerged from the beauty parlor — but my aroma was probably worse than his.

"If you smell an offensive odor," I said, "it's probably me. I've been hiking and haven't had a bath in several days."

"You both stink," she said, stomping off behind the counter.

In a feeble effort to diffuse the tension, I grabbed Gary by the shoulders and said, "If you think *I* smell bad, you ought to smell *him!*"

No one in the place thought it was funny, except Sally.

When I heard the owner tell her regular customers to take up the tables so I wouldn't have a place to sit, I couldn't believe it. It was the blind/deaf treatment all over again, and it made me mad. By law, dog guides have a right to take their masters into any public place and remain there with them. *Any* public place. A lot of people made great personal sacrifices to get that law passed and I wasn't about to back away from it. I figured we'd just have to endure making a scene.

I offered to call the police, but the owner reserved the privilege for herself and promised that her *friend,* the sheriff, would come and take me away.

I'd been arrested for the same thing several times before, so I tackled my hot dog, determined not to go to jail on an empty stomach.

I don't mind telling you I was plenty worried.

The roads were seldom paved out this far in the back country where there are only tiny towns — little settlements, really — so before I finished my last french fry, I could hear this big car come sliding up to the restaurant, shooting gravel everywhere.

The sheriff strutted in — I could hear his footsteps — and boomed, "Where is he, Miz Travis[1]?" Then he clomped over to my table.

I thought I was sunk.

Still, I identified myself.

He said, "Looks like the lady don't want you in here."

Out of my backpack, I pulled a book that I carried with me for just such an emergency, and said, "Sir, would you mind looking at the section of the law pertaining to the state of Virginia?"

I'd never heard such grunting and groaning and carrying-on in my life as I heard while that man read. At most, the passage should take ten seconds to read. It took this sheriff at least two full minutes — making sound effects as he went. And it seemed like thirty minutes to me.

Finally, he said, "Uh oh."

He slapped the book down on the table and hollered, "We're in a heap o' trouble heah, Miz Travis!"

He then took the book to the store owner and told her she would have to let me stay. "According to the law," he said, "you can't evict this man and his dog even if you decide to close up and go home."

After the sheriff left, the lady apologized to me and burst into tears. I held my hand out and she took it.

"I'm real sorry this had to happen," I said, "but it seemed to be the only way."

I had pressed the issue because of the blind people who would come into her place after me. If I had left without standing up for what was right, it would have made it harder for each one of them. We hugged each other and I told her that God loved her and so did I.

---

[1] Not her real name.

I didn't get a chance to hug the sheriff, but I appreciated his willingness to enforce the law. And I appreciated the loyalty of Sally and Gary. They didn't have to stick around for the fireworks, but they stayed with me and never batted an eye. I guess that's what families are all about.

It probably wouldn't be the last time I'd have to fight the same battle. I'd already done it several times. And each time that sense of "family" had helped me out.

Once in my home town of Burlington, the owner of a seafood restaurant had tried to throw me and my dog out. When we wouldn't leave, he swore out a warrant for my arrest and I had to go to jail. I had to sign an appearance bond before I could get out. Then my friends went to work.

The restaurant owner almost lost his business in the days ahead, there was so much public support for us. The story ended up in the newspapers and on the editorial pages for weeks. Eventually the owner had to pay all the legal fees and court costs, publicly apologize, and invite me back to the restaurant as an honored guest.

A similar event nearly got me arrested in South Carolina in 1986, when I was doing some charity work for a firemen's association. And again, after my friends got wind of it, it made the papers.

The third time was in Kinston, North Carolina, where a friend of mine and I tried to get something to eat in a small diner. They wouldn't serve us, and I finally offered to call the police. Thirty minutes later, three policemen roared up. It turned out that all three were African-American police officers. Not very long ago, *they* couldn't have eaten in a small southern diner like that, either, so they were very helpful. It didn't take them long to set the owner straight! Once again, my friend sat steadfastly by me.

That sense of family became one of the most compelling reasons for me to continue walking the A.T.

Each shelter had its own register, which was the closest thing on the Trail to a family album. A spiral notebook, usually protected by a resealable plastic bag and lying on a roof timber, the register served as a Trail newspaper, message board, personal diary, and soapbox for hikers. Notations ranged from a name, date, and "I was here," to a full page on the hiker's philosophy of life. The registers were the heart of the very effective Trail communication network.

After several weeks of listening to the entries of hikers ahead of me, I felt like I knew them before we ever met. Some were crusaders like Linda, the Hunger Hiker, and Larry, the Pro-Lifer. Others were out for a good time. All were part of the family, with their own distinctive personalities and styles.

Cruise Control was committed to taking his time along the way. The Moseys and the Total Recs were fun-loving couples who brought laughter wherever they showed up. The Meyers Brothers slept till noon, then hiked late and woke up everyone in the shelter when they arrived. Van-Go filled the registers with hilarious drawings of his daily experiences and feelings.

I never knew his real name, but I felt a special empathy with Van-Go. (I didn't know it at the time, but he walked with a pronounced limp.) He must have felt a little something for me, too, because he left me quite a few illustrations. He has a great sense of humor and people tell me he is a wonderful artist.

Much later and further north, when I was alone much of the time, the registers were a source of melancholy for me as well. When I was alone, I couldn't read them, so I never knew about the jokes, comments, warnings, or inspirational messages that were left before me.

Every March, a new register is taken to each shelter. A hiker can leave a message that says, "On November 1, will the last person through here mail this register to me?" and some kind of reward is usually offered. (I offered a twenty-five-dollar gift certificate.) Sometimes they're placed by the stiles in fences where the thru-hikers are known to cross over. Each time my hand ran over one, I'd stop and put an entry into it. I could tell with my fingers where the last entry was written and go to the next open spot.

I did get a few registers sent to me after the hike, each full of messages. I treasure them all, like family letters.

Of course, like any family, there were also differences of opinion, and not everyone got along.

One of the issues that tended to divide hikers was the mice that lived in every shelter. These little creatures had discovered that instead of having to forage for food, they could sleep all day and wait for the hikers to bring it to them! These mice were bold, aggressive, and persistent in their chosen way of life. Sometimes they didn't wait for the last candle to be blown out before they went after the food. The only way to beat them was to keep all provisions out of their reach.

Most hikers carried food in a small nylon stuff sack which could be hung from a crossbeam at the front of the shelter. Sometimes that wasn't enough. A skilled mouse could traverse the beam, shinny down the drawstring, and gnaw his way into the sack. The unsuspecting or forgetful hiker who left food in a pack or coat pocket would wake up to find shredded nylon and a precious candy bar partially eaten.

Most hikers adopted a live-and-let-live attitude toward the mice, but others were determined to leave each shelter with fewer rodents than when they arrived. Ray and Louise traveled under the Trail name Special Forces, and waged serious war against the mice. They carried traps and set them in strategic places almost immediately after arriving at a shelter. Before departing, they would add several marks to the mouse body count in the register.

One evening, Peter Martel — Mr. Moleskin — and I were eating our supper along with Ray and Louise. Suddenly there was a loud *snap* overhead, and a mouse caught in a trap fell right into Moleskin's macaroni and cheese! Louise grabbed the trap, held it up like a trophy and cackled, "Look at his little eyes!"

Moleskin came completely unglued and turned the air blue with his view of the Special Forces and their war on rodents.

A father-and-son hiking team once found a mouse suspended in a shelter firepit with a hangman's noose and a neatly tied satin bow around his neck. It was the work of the Meyers Brothers, who had decided that "even a mouse deserved to be buried in a suit." In the middle of the Great Mouse Debate, the father-and-son team introduced an element of humor for people on both sides of the burning issue. Every day or so, they carved a tiny, wooden club about an inch and a half long with a hole in the end of the handle and a little string loop attached. After staying at a shelter, they left the little club hanging by a nail. Underneath were a set of instructions:

Humane Mouse Knocker (pat. pend.)
First, strike mouse firm blow on left temple.
Carry anesthetized mouse to RR and lay on track.
Resulting long, very thin strip of mouse jerky may
be salted, rolled and carried with Trail supplies —
delicious!

In addition to their different attitudes toward rodents, members of the Trail family also differed on matters of hiking ethics. A purist wouldn't think of deviating one step from the white-blazed Trail. Others would take a blue-blazed side trail or hitchhike (yellow-blaze) around a difficult section and feel no guilt.

Registers sometimes contained the confessions of hikers who had skipped a portion of the Trail. One man wrote, "Please, somebody, stop me before I blue-blaze again!"

Necessities were simply a matter of personal style. The Geek carried a four-pound cat named Ziggy on a wooden platform on top of his backpack, and four pounds of cat food inside. Steve, a southbound hiker, was carrying a full-size guitar. Another hiker packed a heavy liquid load, rarely arriving at a shelter without a six-pack of beer.

But it was a man who called himself The Irish Goat who provided one of my best moments on the Trail. His dog, Boomer, hit it off with Orient and, for several nights running, we ended up in the same shelter. The Irish Goat had a long, rather unkempt beard and ate everything with a great deal of gusto. In the middle of one night, he started screaming, and I thought he had been attacked by a bear. Flashlights came on, everyone woke up, and he finally managed to calm down long enough to tell us what happened.

He had eaten spaghetti for supper and gone to bed without washing his face. He awoke in the darkness to find a mouse perched on his chin, eating the spaghetti out of his mustache! He backhanded the poor mouse clear across the shelter.

Thru-hikers are a different breed. They need a compelling reason to abandon the normal creature comforts for six months in order to walk farther than most people drive on a family vacation. Since it probably takes one to know one, almost everything I discovered about "them" also applied to me.

One of my first surprises was how little thru-hikers talked about their lives in the "real" world. Campfire conversations rarely included any mention of a person's job. It was something most hikers seemed content to leave in the background. The Trail — what you had completed and what lay ahead — occupied most conversations at the end of a day.

Food was another big item in the family. For most of us, this was the first legal food binge of our lives. We needed six thousand calories a day just to keep up with what we were burning on the Trail. Enormous servings of pasta, or noodles laced with liquid margarine, were the usual fare for dinner. The expensive, dehydrated "yuppie dinners" containing meat were a rare treat. A craving for fresh fruit and vegetables built to near obsession between towns.

The amount we ate in restaurants could only be described as shameful. Five thru-hikers could devastate an entire all-you-can-eat salad bar. I left a couple of places feeling like I had participated in an act of destruction worse than Sherman's march through Georgia. The restaurants must have had people other than hikers in mind when they said it was all-you-can-eat.

Of course, not everything was light-hearted on the Trail.

I was eight miles outside Erwin, Tennessee, which is a big stop for thru-hikers, and I was anxious to get into town. The Trail along here is very narrow and slippery at the best of times and it had been raining a lot. The Trail was also pretty narrow, and banked or slanted away from the mountain-side down into a big opening, almost a small valley, some fifty to sixty feet below.

The footing was plenty treacherous for me, particularly in the narrower parts, which were only six inches wide or less. Since Orient and I walk side-by-side, we really needed more room. Whenever Orient was on the outside, he kept sliding off — not that I was particularly sure-footed myself.

Finally, we came to a place where the Trail virtually disappeared. At that moment, Orient stopped. But I didn't.

Over the side of the mountain I slid!

When something like this happens, your natural response is to flail your hands wildly to grab something or to brace yourself for the fall.

And that's what happened.

Precisely where I fell, there was a little sapling. I grabbed it so unerringly, it was almost as if I could see it.

It saved me for a moment, till one of the thru-hikers behind us saw what happened, rushed forward, and grabbed me by the pack, pulling me to safety.

Now, some people saw a coincidence in that sapling being just where I could blindly grab it. Not me.

One of the sensational supermarket tabloids found out about the incident and ran a story saying I was dangling from mid-air, holding on by one finger and screaming, "Oh God, please don't let me die!"

As a matter of fact, dying never entered my mind; it wasn't even close. I didn't have time to think. But what really happened was just as miraculous.

On May 5, Anna Vail joined me in Damascus, Virginia, planning to hike the next fifty miles. I'd met her a year and a half earlier. She worked at the National Institute of Health in Bethesda, Maryland, and was a friend of my daughter. She was interested in outdoor activities, got caught up in the whole hiking thing, and became part of my support group.

I was with Gary, Steve, Sally and some others when Anna joined us. On the second day of her hike, Anna slipped on some wet straw in the rain. Her legs went out from under her and she landed awkwardly. It broke a bone and she started screaming in pain.

We made a splint out of her foam rubber mattress and wrapped her entire leg. Steve heard a car in the distance, so we figured a road must be fairly close by. I stayed with Anna while Steve went crashing through the woods for help. When Anna began to get cold, I set up my tent by the Trail to get her out of the wind and rain.

It seemed that Steve was gone for hours. We prayed a lot, sang songs, told jokes about the Trail and did anything we could think of to distract Anna from the pain.

Meanwhile, Steve had found the road and hitchhiked the twenty-eight road miles back to Damascus. He was directed to the fire department's rescue squad, which just happened to be participating in a seminar conducted by people from another town. There were thirty rescue people there, and when Steve burst in and announced our plight, they all thought it was a plan instigated by the instructors. It happened to be at the most appropriate time in the seminar!

Back at the scene of Anna's accident, we heard all this noise down the Trail and the sound of vehicles nearby. We were quickly surrounded by people, all rushing up to us at the same time.

It turned out that my tent was on an old trail that led right to the road, just a quarter of a mile away. So the rescuers organized three teams of six people to carry Anna out that way and on to the closest major hospital, in Bristol, Tennessee. Steve and I got a hotel room and stayed there until Anna's leg was set and her mother came to take her home.

We arrived back on the Trail at about 1:00 p.m. the following day, still carrying Anna's food, which happened to include some steaks. We were salivating at the thought of enjoying that meat. After walking 150 yards on the Trail, we came upon a beautiful pond, where a couple of men were fishing. After talking to them for awhile, it began to look like rain, so we called it a day and cooked those steaks.

What had started out to be a twelve-mile day became a 150-yard day!

Because hikers are a mobile community, there were usually never more than a few of us in the same place at the same time. One big exception was the annual Trail Days Festival in Damascus, Virginia, a place many call the friendliest town on the A.T.

During late May, several hundred people converged for a big reunion and celebration. There were about one hundred of the current year's thru-hikers, and twenty-five who had completed the hike the year before. We all walked together in the Trail Days parade, along with a pot-and-pan marching band. And in the middle of us was Orient with his head held high, taking in all the sights and sounds.

That weekend may have been the first time I fully realized how much of a family we had become. We greeted each other like long-lost friends and shared Trail talk until the wee hours. Whenever Orient recognized friends from the Trail, he got excited and started whining and wagging his tail. They had lots of pats and ear-scratches for Orient and he loved that.

The Sunday evening talent show was hilarious, with a lot of hikers performing skits and songs. One thru-hiker known as "The Hobbit," stole the show with his song about M&M's:

> *It's a bright little 'pill' you carry in your pack,*
> *Comes in all colors, and makes a good snack.*
> *Eat 'em in the morning, eat 'em at night,*
> *Any time you eat 'em makes you feel all right.*
> *Hey, I'm singin' about 'Emmies,' 'Emmies,'*
> *Bright little happy 'pills.'*
> *Can't do the Trail without 'em,*
> *Cures up all your ills... 'cept maybe giardia.*

Almost before we'd stopped laughing about that, Hobbit sang a beautiful ballad about his father, who had introduced him to the A.T. as a child. This made me think about my dad and how much I missed him. I hoped it was okay for thru-hikers to cry.

One of the mysteries of growing up was becoming a father while I was still a son. Even with children of my own, there was a little-boy part of me that lived on in a kind of endless childhood. Whenever I was with my father, I always felt about nine years old, and listened carefully for some reassurance from him that I was doing okay. When he died, I tried to comfort my children while the little boy inside me felt crushed and bewildered.

I often wondered what my own kids really thought about me. I had done enough to be disowned by every one of them, but they had somehow managed to stand by me with a lot of love and support. Billy and Jonathan had spent the weekend with me in Erwin, Tennessee, and later all the kids met me near Bastian, Virginia. It was wonderful to hear their voices and be together for a couple of days. I prayed a lot for them as I walked the Trail each day, and I asked God to make things right in our family and help me be the father I should be.

The last night of Trail Days, Orient and I made our way through the rain back to The Place, a hostel run by the local Methodist church. It was jammed with hikers, and tents were pitched all over the lawn. In the morning, this transient group of shirt-tail relatives would pack up and disappear back onto that mysterious stretch of life we called "the Trail." It was sad to think that many of us would never meet again.

On the other hand, it was fun to anticipate the surprise reunions that lay somewhere ahead.

Trail Days reminded each of us that our hike was not a solo effort. This family we were part of included people on and off the Trail who cared about each other. The weekend in Damascus had been a living picture of that, a wonderful interlude that left me tired, but encouraged.

Chapter Eleven

Becoming Emotionally Lean

After the break for Trail Days, Orient and I, Sally, Gary, and another hiker called Sorefeet resumed the trek. We were planning to meet that night at the Pine Swamp Branch shelter, eighteen miles ahead. Within an hour we were spread out along the Trail, each moving at a different pace. I wasn't making great time, since Orient's pack and mine were heavy with a fresh supply of food, and I was breaking in a new pair of boots.

Late in the afternoon, I passed Sorefeet's tent. He said Sally and the Englishman had gone on to the shelter, so I decided to press on to meet them as we had planned. By 9:30 that night, however, I still had not reached the shelter and it was beginning to rain. Orient must have taken a wrong turn somewhere, because he was showing all the signs of being off the Trail. I decided to camp right where we were.

The only level place was an old roadbed that rejected my every attempt to pound in a peg. I vowed that my next tent would be freestanding. When the drizzle turned to a downpour, I just spread the tent fly over the two of us and we hunkered in for the night. My two water bottles were empty, so Orient drank the rain that was running off the nylon over our heads. I held my bandana outside, then sucked it to relieve my thirst. There wasn't room to eat, so we skipped dinner entirely. We spent a cold, wet, miserable night amidst thunder and driving rain.

What a contrast to Trail Days! Strangers had introduced themselves, congratulated me on my progress, and said they had been wanting to meet me for several weeks! Then, there hadn't seemed to be enough hours in the day to talk to everyone. It had been easy to think I was some kind of guy. Now, less than twenty-four hours later, here I was, lying in a wet sleeping bag next to a shivering dog, trying to relax and get warm enough to go to sleep.

Nights like this seemed to come regularly no matter how hard I worked to avoid them. I wondered how much easier it would be if I wasn't blind. With sight, I could read the maps, step over the rocks and make it to the shelters instead of wandering off the Trail. Sometimes I was amazed at the utter stupidity of what I was trying to do. Lying in a puddle of cold rain, it was hard to see the point of it all.

A couple of days later, I met two hikers at a shelter and we had a very interesting conversation. They said they were going to ask God to restore my sight.

"If God gave you enough faith to come out here and hike the Trail," they said, "surely He will give you enough faith to get your sight back."

They said that they were praying that when I reached the top of Mt. Katahdin, God would miraculously restore my sight so I could do the Trail, sighted, next year. I thanked them for their concern and we went our separate ways.

Was that why God had brought me out here? He was certainly powerful enough to restore my sight. But was that what He *wanted* to do?

I never had any doubts that God had called me to hike the Appalachian Trail. As strange as it must have sounded to others, my sense of being on a Divine mission was solidly confirmed before Orient and I left Springer Mountain.

Without that call, I couldn't and wouldn't have been on the Trail.

But I never pretended to understand His reasons. One part seemed to involve my talking to people along the way. I was always amazed at the deep conversations I had about faith in God. There was something about life on the Trail that created an openness between us.

One instance of this occurred when a man named Phillip[1] began hiking with Orient and me. I knew he had something on his mind. He hinted at it over several days and finally blurted it out one night by the campfire when the two of us were camped alone. A couple of years before, he had had a sexual experience that had left him feeling guilty and confused. Since then, he had been using alcohol to avoid dealing with it. He told me that he felt his life was ruined and that God could never forgive him. He had not told anyone about it before, and I thought it odd that he was telling me.

Strangely enough, as he told me his story and I prayed about how to respond, I knew what I had to tell him. As a child, I had been sexually abused by an adult relative, and was afraid to tell anyone about it. It had left me angry and confused, too. My years of promiscuity had been somehow wrapped up in trying to deal with and overcome that sexual abuse. I had always considered it one of the most unfortunate and damaging experiences of my life.

But that evening by the campfire, I began to see it in a different light.

As I shared my story with Phillip, I could feel the pain going away from both of us. I told him there was no sin God wouldn't forgive if we truly repented and confessed it to Him. He could even take the tragedies of our lives and bring good from them.

And He did. That night, God took an experience that had haunted me since childhood and used it to help a young

---

[1] Not his real name.

man struggling with similar feelings of guilt and shame. Out of the garbage of my life, He made something good.

The next day, I could hear a difference in Phillip's voice, and he walked as if his pack were twenty pounds lighter. A few days later, he said good-bye and hiked ahead on his own.

I found that a heavy burden had been lifted from my heart as well.

Time isn't supposed to be a problem in the wilderness, but it became one whenever I thought about how many miles there were between me and Mt. Katahdin. Sharing my faith was part of the call to walk the A.T., but completing the trek was the other part. That meant crossing paths with lots of hikers who had time to say little more than a hello.

As the hike progressed, I sensed another dimension of the wilderness — the ability to spend time alone with God. Away from the noise and distractions of my normal life, I had a unique opportunity to listen. I hadn't requested this experience, so He must have known that I needed it. He also must have known how long it would take me to hear what He was trying to say.

During the day, hiking required almost one hundred percent of my concentration. But the nights alone gave me a lot of time for thinking and praying. Instead of a few minutes of silence each day, there were often hours. I talked to God a lot about my family, fellow hikers, and friends at home. So many were struggling with questions that seemed to have no answers.

Like most thru-hikers, I alternated between craving human companionship and wanting to be alone. After a few days of hiking with people and sleeping in crowded shelters, I often pitched my tent away from the others just to savor the peace and quiet of isolation.

But some hikers seemed almost afraid of solitude. Several people wore headphones all day, listening to tapes or the radio. One man in Georgia carried a battery-powered

TV so he wouldn't miss the NCAA basketball finals. Most hikers enjoyed the quiet, but it was surprising how many stayed glued to the TV for hours when they made it to a motel.

I believe there is a certain sense of awe and renewal for anyone who spends much time exposed to nature. For me, the experience on the Trail went far beyond that. It didn't take long to realize that this wonderful wilderness was a tool in God's hands, sometimes gentle and sometimes harsh, to put me in my place.

I had always equated humility with weakness or subservience. I thought "humble" was about the worst thing you could call someone. A meek person wouldn't stand up for his rights, I thought, and I had spent all my life doing that.

On the Trail, I was learning another side of humility. First, I wasn't in charge out here. The weather, the terrain, and the animals were out of my control. This was God's world and He was in charge. My choices were limited: To hike or not to hike; to accept or reject; to cooperate or complain.

At home, if I didn't like the temperature, I could change it with a switch. I lived and worked mostly indoors and could easily control that small environment. Out here, it was completely out of my hands. But all of us hiking the Trail had chosen to limit our options in order to expand our experience. I was learning to let go.

I was also learning that I simply could not hike the Trail without the help and protection of God. Some days I must have fallen fifty times, and every time I went down, I tried to thank Him that I wasn't hurt badly and that Orient was okay. Every fall slowed me down and reminded me how vulnerable I was. Without those falls, I could have developed an unbearable pride in my own abilities.

The big boulders and fallen trees rarely caused me to fall. Most often, it was a small rock that turned my ankle, or a thin root that caught my toe when I was trying to walk too fast on a fairly level stretch of ground.

Humility came with having to ask people for the kind of help I had never needed before. During an early stopover in Hiawassee, Georgia, with a hiker named Jeff, I had only a small amount of cash on me and the motels wouldn't take credit cards. A man at the post office suggested we call a local church and ask if we could sleep in their basement or pitch a tent on the lawn.

They turned us down flat saying, "We have no provision to help people like you."

Glen Eller, a man who overheard the phone conversation, paid for our motel room that night and took Jeff and me to church with him the next morning. When he told the congregation who I was and why I was hiking the Trail, they took up a love offering — which embarrassed me to death. I finally convinced Glen that I was only short of cash, not destitute. I asked if they could use the offering to start a fund to help other people who were stranded in town, and they agreed.

I liked being the help-er, not the help-ee.

But on the Trail, there were scores of situations where I couldn't make it without the help of others. In the wilderness, I wasn't in charge. I wasn't in control. And I certainly wasn't capable of handling everything by myself. Because of this, many people along the way helped me learn a new dimension of faith through their generosity and love. I came to see my contact with every person as a divinely arranged appointment in which my job was to fit in with God's purpose for bringing us together.

In some places, the Appalachian Trail is only a ribbon through developed areas of homes and businesses. In other places, it is in the midst of the wilderness. When you're blind, it can be hard to tell the difference.

One day, I was hiking along thinking that God, Orient, and I were the only ones within miles. I was startled to hear a voice from a loudspeaker say, "Will Jim Davis please come to the telephone?"

I laughed to think that this part of my wilderness Trail was only a narrow corridor bordered by the back lots of businesses and warehouses. Other hikers were more aware of the proximity of urban areas because they saw the lights of the houses and cities at night. It took the man-made noises to bring the reality of civilization home to me.

With enough money, a person could spend almost as many nights in motels as in tents or shelters along the Trail. Some nights it seemed ridiculous to lie in a tent with cold, hurting feet when I could hear the noise of traffic on a highway and knew that a bathtub full of hot water was only minutes away.

But after a while, I began to realize that my place of testing was more than geographical. There was the growing problem of media attention and the danger of my becoming addicted to the praise people kept heaping on me. I also felt the pressure of time and the need to finish my trek. Sometimes the sheer physical pain of hiking made me want to sit down and cry.

What was I doing in this wilderness, anyway?

June 6 was Orient's third birthday, so I gave him some "cookies" and sang *Happy Birthday* to him in the morning. He enjoyed the Milkbones more than the music. I said a special prayer of thanks for him and left messages in a couple of shelters announcing his birthday.

A couple of weeks later I reached Harpers Ferry, West Virginia, where the Shenandoah River joins forces with the Potomac for its final push to the Atlantic. A lot of pretty important people had crossed ahead of me — George Washington, Robert E. Lee, and John Brown, along with many others.

Even though Harpers Ferry was a little less than halfway to Katahdin, it was the psychological mid-point for most northbound hikers. Stopping at the Appalachian

Trail Conference headquarters and having my picture made for the thru-hiker scrapbook was a significant milestone.

At the ATC office, I spent a good bit of time studying their relief map of the entire Trail. I ran my fingers over every inch of it, reviewing the portion I had covered and trying to imagine what the terrain was like ahead. The level portions appeared deceptively easy, because I knew the map couldn't show the sharp rocks in Pennsylvania or the bogs in Maine. All the mountains, including the notorious White Mountains in New Hampshire, seemed like little bumps compared to Katahdin. It rose straight up out of nothing and dared me to climb it.

Three friends from Burlington joined me in Harpers Ferry, and we hiked together for a couple of days. It was great to catch up on all the news from home, and I admired their willingness to come straight from the office and get right on the Trail. But I was appalled at all the things they had brought for a twenty-mile trek. Their packs reminded me of the one I had lugged to Neels Gap — two of everything and enough food for a month. It was hard to watch their pack weight robbing their strength and enjoyment of the Trail, but hiking seemed to be the only way any of us came to understand the burden of possessing too much.

They noticed that I'd lost some weight, but I told them it was nothing compared to the "emotional fat" — all the things I thought I could never do without — that had melted away along the Trail. For some people, shedding emotional fat consisted of hitchhiking into Trail towns and asking for free leftover food at restaurants. For others, it was going two weeks between showers and wearing the same clothes day after day.

Speaking of wearing the same clothes... The fellows enjoyed my description of doing laundry. To cut down the weight of my pack, I wore all my hiking clothes and mailed my church clothes ahead to selected towns along the Trail. When I couldn't stand my clothes any longer, I would put on my poncho, peel off all my clothes under it, and stroll into a laundromat. It was a trick I'd learned from a veteran thru-hiker. I did this in a little town one hot, sunny day, and a lady in the laundromat asked me what I had on under the poncho. Obviously I wasn't wearing it for warmth! I just laughed, although I'm not sure a real *lady* would ask a question like that!

I'm glad I wore an olive drab poncho, rather than a clear plastic one!

Other things that changed as I shed my emotional fat concerned general hygiene. Before my hike, I wouldn't ever let Orient drink from my cup. Now, I laugh as I recall the night I rinsed out his plastic food bowl and used it to serve salad to another hiker. Other creature comforts went by the way, too. Bathing in icy streams, using outhouses, and hiking day after day in the rain were now commonplace.

While I didn't necessarily relish some of my experiences on the hike, they helped cement my belief that nothing was going to happen to me that wasn't supposed to happen. Some people thought I was trying to test God by walking the A.T. But that was just not so! I was very aware that hiking through electrical storms with a metal pole in my right hand made me a lightning rod. In fact, for the first five hundred miles, I kept the prayer line hot whenever the rains came and the thunder rolled. But I wasn't some kind of daredevil. I didn't get any pleasure from close calls or dangerous situations. After a while, I decided He knew where I was and what was going on. I still had to use good judgment, but I didn't have to live in fear.

I also discovered that, for the most part, I tended to worry about the wrong things. Instead of thinking about being struck by lightning or attacked by a bear, I needed to focus on my attitude. Was I thanking God for my circumstances or complaining about them? It seemed that God's protection and guidance were easier to see in matters of life and death than they were in little everyday situations.

So the wilderness became a place of revelation for me. Every day, I saw more of who I was and what I was really like. Much of that was unpleasant and hard to take. If that had been all there was, it would have left me completely discouraged.

But every day, I saw more of God's faithfulness and care.

Chapter Twelve

More Lessons Learned

Mornings began slowly in every Trail shelter along the A.T. Before daylight, one or two people usually emerged from their sleeping bags and shouldered their packs with hardly a sound. They were the mega-hikers who covered five miles before pausing in the first rays of the sun for a candy bar or a cup of tea. They might log another twenty-five miles before unrolling their sleeping bags that evening. The next morning they would do the same. They always said good-bye at night, because in the morning the only farewell they got was a chorus of snores.

Meanwhile, back in the shelter, it would be another hour before I awoke to the sounds of sleeping-bag zippers, the rustle of nylon, whispers, groans, and the familiar crunch of hands groping inside food bags for a packet of oatmeal, noodles, or cocoa. At the front of the shelter, I heard water trickle into a pot, followed by the sputtering of vaporized fuel, a whoosh of ignition, and the reassuring hiss of a small stove burning with a hot blue flame.

One thru-hiker described his typical morning like this:
– Wake up from dreaming that I'm on the beach at Cancun.
– Close my eyes and try to restart the dream.
– Fail.

– Realize I *must* visit the privy immediately.
– Remember it is a quarter of a mile away through the
    drizzle and fog.
– Consider what will happen if I don't leave this instant.
– Exit bag, don clammy T-shirt and shorts, hobble over
    rocks and roots, only to find privy occupied by a
    weekend hiker reading *The Sunday New York Times*.
– Look for a log in the woods.
– Try to remember why I'm doing this to myself.

One advantage I had over most other thru-hikers was
that I had never enjoyed hiking. Backpacking had never
appealed to me even when I was sighted. It just didn't fit
my idea of a good time. After getting my first Seeing Eye
dog, I walked five to ten miles a day for transportation, not
for exercise or recreation. Walking was simply a means to
an end. I felt much the same way about the Trail.

Most other hikers had different expectations. Those
who had enjoyed weekend or longer treks started out
ecstatic about spending six months on the Trail. It sounded
like heaven. Many set out believing that every day would
be an exhilarating experience of inner renewal in an
unspoiled woodland. Instead of listening to office gossip
and the sterile "bloop" of the air bubble in a water bottle,
they would hear the birds and drink their fill alone from a
gurgling stream.

The initial euphoria sometimes lasted a week or a
month, but then the newness wore off and the monotony set
in. Mountains began to look alike, the absence of creature
comforts became a nuisance instead of a challenge, and the
joy of solitude gave way to loneliness and a craving for
family and old friends.

If variety is the spice of life, then routine is salt that has
lost its savor.

For every thru-hiker, there was a point when walking
the A.T. stopped being fun and started being work. It was
different for each person. I could almost tell by someone's

voice when hiking stopped being a hobby and turned into a job.

It happened to me when I took my first step on the Trail. A little cabana on the beach at Waikiki would have seemed like recreation, but walking two thousand miles of mountainous terrain with a heavy pack was definitely a job.

Initially, I couldn't see the psychological advantage in starting with this attitude, but it became clear as I went along. Since I never expected hiking to be fun, I wasn't disillusioned when it felt like work. Neither was the weather a surprise.

Warren Doyle's A.T. weather prediction for a thru-hike was: eighty percent of the time, it's either too wet, too dry, too hot, or too cold; twenty percent of the time it's just right. He said the sooner we got used to the fact that only one day out of five would be good weather, the happier we'd be. Somehow, it was hard not to wish for more. I found that my serenity was inversely proportional to my expectations.

The comic strip character Pogo is best remembered for saying, "We have met the enemy and he is us." That's the way it was on the A.T. The enemy was not the Trail, the rocks or the weather — it was ourselves. All the thru-hikers I met fought a constant battle to keep from hating what they had set out to enjoy.

Most people who abandoned their thru-hike did so because it didn't make sense to keep punishing themselves by hiking day after day, often in rain and cold. They said things like, "I'm just not having fun any more" or "The Trail isn't meeting my needs."

I didn't blame them a bit. Without a clear sense of mission, I couldn't have kept going in the face of recurring hardships that I did my best to avoid.

A few days out of Harpers Ferry, two friends, Laurie and Dick, took my pack in the morning and agreed to meet me that afternoon at a shelter up the Trail. Through a series

of mix-ups, we missed each other, and I continued hiking
past the shelter. By the time I realized what had happened,
Orient and I were in the middle of a difficult boulder field
known as Devils Racecourse, and it was getting dark.
When Orient could no longer find the Trail, I decided we
had to stop for the night.

I wrapped up in my poncho and shared the last pint of
water with Orient. Instead of a restful night in a shelter with
friends, we were stuck in the rocks without the food and
water we needed. Several people would be worried about
us and would probably be out searching through the night.

Suddenly, I heard a rattling sound nearby. Did they
have snakes up here? Could a curious rattlesnake be
inspecting our campsite?

A few months before, I would have been frustrated
and started asking a lot of questions: "If hiking this Trail is
my job, why can't I do it better? Why does what I am doing
seem to require so much help from others? Where was God
when I passed that shelter? What is the point in keeping a
lot of people awake looking for us?"

Oddly enough, none of those things was in my mind
that night. It was one of those rare moments when I could
see the growth and change in me since starting on the Trail.
I asked the Lord to keep Orient and me safe and to help the
people who might be out looking for us. I was finally
learning to trust.

There were days when I was thrilled with the beauty
of creation. There were other times when God's world
seemed far from perfect. I was finally learning to take the
good with the bad and to accept the weather and terrain for
what they were, instead of wishing they conformed to my
desires.

I had discovered that hiking the Trail was like being a
guest in someone else's home. My Host controlled the
thermostat and arranged the furniture the way He wanted
it. His invitation was, "Make yourself at home."

On July 1, a sweltering Sunday, I reached Pine Grove Furnace, Pennsylvania, and stood beside a sign with arrows pointing north to Katahdin and south to Springer Mountain. The distance to both was the same — 1,069 miles.

I was really halfway there — after nearly four months on the Trail!

Part of Trail tradition at the halfway point was joining "The Half-Gallon Club." This involved buying a half-gallon of Heavenly Hash ice cream. I ate the whole thing in twenty minutes. It tasted so good, I bought another one and took my time with it. Orient had a "cookie" and a big bowl of water, then promptly went to sleep in the nearest shade.

The rocks in Pennsylvania had the reputation for being the sharpest along the A.T. Some people accused the local residents of sharpening them during the winter and gleefully awaiting the next season's crop of hikers. The combination of rocks and heat was particularly hard on Orient. The leather boots I had made to protect his feet were too hot for the summer weather. But without them, his feet became cut and sore.

Whenever Orient got tired, he let me know and we would stop for a couple of hours, or sometimes the rest of the day. Frequently, people asked me how many dogs I'd been through on the Trail. They thought Orient was the third or fourth. One person even called the Seeing Eye and asked why they were delivering new dogs to me on the Trail.

But Orient was the one and only. We started together in Georgia, and I prayed every day that we'd be able to cross the finish line together in Maine.

At Duncannon, Pennsylvania, a vet examined Orient and said he was in excellent health, except for the pads of his feet. He recommended five days of complete rest so they could heal completely. I was ready for a break myself. The afternoons and nights off the Trail never seemed long enough to get rested. I hadn't realized how much both of us needed an extended physical and mental break.

Orient had lost some weight, so I increased his rations to three pounds of high-performance dog food a day. That would give him nine thousand calories daily. Anybody ought to be able to gain weight on that. My calorie consumption was already about as high as it could get, so I just kept on enjoying all the ice cream I could find.

For the better part of a week, I sat by the swimming pool and didn't do much of anything while Orient slept at least eighteen hours a day.

One afternoon, I had eaten a whole package of beef jerky, and was halfway through a second, when my host, Tim Boyer, walked over and asked what I was eating. I offered him some jerky and handed him the package. He laughed, gave it back and informed me that the label said "Doggie Treats." They had been sent to me by two hikers known as The Blister Sisters, and I thought they were pretty good!

I gave Orient the ones I hadn't eaten and apologized for stealing his food.

In towns all along the A.T., children provided some of my favorite moments. They always seemed so honest and open and unafraid to ask questions about my blindness. They wanted to know how I could tell a five dollar bill from a ten dollar bill, how I found the things I dropped on the ground, and who told me what color my clothes were.

The kids, especially the little ones, enjoyed Orient, too. In Duncannon, Tim and Debbie Boyer's five-year-old daughter, Emily, loved Orient and called him "Oreo." Orient fell in love with Emily, too, following her around wherever she went. The day we left, she cried when she told Orient good-bye.

The week-long hiatus in Duncannon was good for Orient's feet and for his spirit, too. When we returned to the Trail, he walked with a more determined step than ever before. It was impossible to know what he was thinking, but I got the distinct impression that he was beginning to enjoy all this.

Seventy miles up the Trail, I walked into Port Clinton, Pennsylvania, on a Saturday afternoon and thought I'd entered The Twilight Zone. I knew I was in a town, but there didn't seem to be anyone around. After knocking on half a dozen doors and getting no answer, I yelled out, "Doesn't anyone live here?" A boy answered and said, "I do."

Matthew was eight years old and out for a bike ride. He said things were so quiet because most people had driven to Allentown to shop. When I asked directions to the public pavilion in the park, he volunteered to show me the way. We had a nice talk as he pedaled slowly along beside Orient and me.

The Pennsylvania rocks finally got to me several days out of Port Clinton. Those rocks are made of shale and there are a lot of them. They're not large, only about twice the size of a fist, but they make the footing treacherous. What's worse, they move when you step on them!

Other rocks are neither round nor flat, but rather shaped like blunted arrowheads, it's very easy to twist and turn your ankle. A lot of them stick two or three inches out of the Trail — and that's just what's exposed. The roots go all the way to the center of the earth!

I know because, after falling one time, I tried to beat or break one of them down. It didn't budge. So when you step — or fall — these rocks are like spikes in a board — they're murder on your feet and ankles.

In this part of Pennsylvania, much of the A.T. goes across huge tracts of land, giant plateaus that stretch for miles with only slight ups and downs, vast areas with just a few trees and a little scrub brush. There used to be some pretty good forests here, but the trees were so riddled by gypsy moths that they were completely defoliated by the worms. And everywhere are these deep, embedded rocks. By the end of the day, your ankles are double their natural size from all the twisting and contorting they've had to do.

Naturally, it was along here that my feet slipped on a rocky portion of the Trail. I landed on my chest, and the weight of my pack drove me into a sharp rock. I knew immediately that I'd cracked a rib. I managed to carry my pack for the rest of the day, to where I had arranged to meet my friend, Anna, at a road crossing. Despite the broken leg she had suffered on the Trail in Virginia, Anna managed to shuttle my pack ahead by car for several days. That way, I could keep hiking and give the rib time to heal.

It seemed like all the hikers hit a lull once they left Pennsylvania and began to trek up through New Jersey, New York, and into New England — and I was no exception. It was hot and humid. People stayed around the shelters later in the morning and stopped hiking earlier in the evenings. Some days, even the most dedicated didn't go anywhere at all.

Some hikers even became lackadaisical about eating. It struck me as funny to hear people complain about eating "the same old thing, day after day" when they were cooking for themselves. Early on, I had determined never to get bored with my food. I carried small portions of chili powder, garlic powder, onion flakes, seasoning salt, and a small bottle of tabasco. Whenever possible, I bought a big, fresh onion to keep things interesting.

Many nights, I asked other hikers to give me one food item from their pack. Then I combined them all into a stew. If someone had a can of tomato sauce, we were really in great shape. They had their doubts at first, but soon discovered I didn't have to be able to see to cook!

In August, the comings and goings of hikers became more pronounced than ever with people taking off a week here and two weeks there, then getting back on the Trail. Because of this, I began running into people I hadn't seen since way back in Virginia. After being ahead of me for weeks, they were just catching up again after an extended break. It was always great to recognize familiar voices and hear about adventures that happened since we last talked.

After struggling 550 miles through Virginia and 230 miles through Pennsylvania, the next few state lines were fun to click off: ninety miles in New Jersey; seventy-three miles in New York; fifty miles in Connecticut; eighty-eight miles in Massachusetts. It was exciting to cover four states in four weeks, but it was a deceptive measure of my progress.

As we went through New Jersey, the Trail started to run on paved roads. The thru-hikers' biggest concern now, rather than falling off a mountain, was how to avoid being run over by a car. (There are still a few of these road walks left on the A.T., particularly in Sussex County, New Jersey, despite a big push to eliminate all of them.)

I spent a couple of days on the roads in New Jersey and in the Kittatinny Mountains. Just as I'd begin to think I was invisible amid all of the people and cars, reporters would come out and interview me. They were from all over the place — New Jersey, New York, even Pennsylvania. And, the day after their stories would hit the papers, people would come out to see me. Some brought their home video cameras, some came bringing lemonade or soft drinks. One guy even brought beer, figuring that a former alcoholic needed it more than most!

There were even people who would shout as they zoomed by. "Hi Bill!" they'd yell, "Keep it up!" Other people would walk along the road with Orient and me for a few minutes and say things like, "We've been following you since you left Georgia." It's a great experience to be all alone on the road and have someone drive by and call out your name. I had a real warm feeling of belonging in New Jersey.

While I was in that state, I made a trip to The Seeing Eye in Morristown, where I had dinner with a committee that questioned me about Orient's treatment. I tried to answer all of their questions. They'd heard some awful rumors about what was happening to Orient — some newspapers had even said I was abusing him. They wanted to see first-hand that he was in good health.

At the time, Orient was thin again, and I was a little concerned myself. But the experience at The Seeing Eye was positive and, after they were sure he was in good health, I left with the feeling that they were supporting what I was doing. Before, I hadn't known.

In New York, I remember sitting in the wilderness one evening, hearing the other hikers discuss the skyline of New York City. Had they not told me, the sounds were my only clue that we were in industrial states like New York and New Jersey. In many places, the A.T. corridor parallels major roads. The sounds of the birds would be drowned out by trucks wheeling down the interstate. That was probably the most disappointing sound on the Trail. It reminded me of how close I was to the very densely populated portion of the country.

I could also tell when there were a lot of road crossings in a mile stretch. We'd be going along peacefully only to discover we were in a thin patch of woods next to a four-lane highway.

But the best thing about New York were the three days I spent at Graymoor Monastery. Father Joe Egan, the monastery's public relations director, had contacted my friend and support team leader, Carolyn Starling, long before I ever got to New York. Through her, he invited me to spend time at the monastery. As Franciscans, part of their call was to take in travelers, so they always fed thru-hikers and put them up for the night. Since they perceived that what I was out doing was what they were doing, they sent me a special invitation.

When I finally arrived, they not only sent out an entourage to meet me, but a TV crew from the Fox Network was there as well! I was introduced to both Father Egan and Father Boscoe, who took care of the thru-hikers for the monastery.

Now, I'd never met a real, live monk before, so my perception of one was of a dried-up little old man, wearing a scratchy hood, and walking around drafty halls saying nothing. I was curious about what they were wearing, so I decided that, rather than shake hands, I would hug them when we were introduced. And that's what I did.

To my surprise, I could tell that Father Egan had on what felt like a nice golf shirt! And when I nonchalantly ran my hand over his head, he had on one of those Ben Hogan-type golf hats! I was shocked!

I said, "Father Egan, you don't have on a monk's uniform."

"Here, feel *him*," Father Egan said as he grabbed Father Boscoe and pulled him over, "Father Boscoe is a *real* monk!"

Instead of being somber and quiet , the men I met were happy, robust and exciting. We quickly became friends.

After the TV crew left, the monks gave me a tour. Orient and I had a private room with a banner across it to welcome us. I realized this was partly because the monks needed some publicity to help raise money, but I had a great time anyway. In fact, we had such a good time that, since I'd just blown out a pair of boots, I ordered another pair and stayed three days and two nights at the monastery waiting for my new boots.

One of the highlights of my stay there was the regular 5:30 p.m. prayer time. When they first invited me to come, I thought, "What a wonderful experience it would be to have forty-eight monks praying for me at one time!" So on the way over there, I decided to ask them to pray specifically for me. But just before I walked in the door, one of the monks whispered, "When we get in here, we'd like you to lead us in prayer, since we figure you've got a closer connection with the Almighty than we do!"

I was flabbergasted! But somehow I muddled through.

The time at the monastery was well spent.

Next came the northwest corner of Connecticut, where we were met by representatives of the Connecticut branch of the Appalachian Mountain Club. They wanted to have a dinner for us at Silver Hill Cabin along the Trail. I arrived with about twelve other thru-hikers — which really strained the food resources of the club.

After dinner, we spent the night in the cabin, which was one of the nicest places on the A.T. It was complete with real doors, rooms, everything! There was even a kitchen and a private bedroom for volunteers, and they gave me the key to those rooms. But by this point I was having trouble sleeping indoors, surrounded by four walls, so I gave the key to a young married couple who had been hiking southbound. They'd been on the Trail for a while and hadn't had any privacy the whole time.

That night, I fell asleep on the deck under a beautiful full moon. I was sound asleep in the middle of the night when a girl left the cabin to go to the privy.

Just as she reached it, a series of blood-curdling screams erupted from the other side of the cabin. I sat bolt upright and was vaguely aware that Orient had disappeared. The screams continued, and I fumbled around the deck to the other side of the cabin.

One voice belonged to Rick (one of the Total Recs). He was in his tent out under the trees, screaming, "Get away from me, bear! Go away!"

When she heard that, the girl in the privy started screaming, too.

The other thru-hikers arrived ahead of me and immediately started laughing. The "bear" was Orient, standing outside the tent, silhouetted through the tent material by the bright full moon. His shadow must have made him look like a big, shaggy bear to Rick, who was probably pretty sleepy. The girl didn't come out until someone assured her there was no bear — just Orient.

Rick has never lived it down.

August 16 was my fiftieth birthday, so I decided to take the day off at Upper Goose Pond in Massachusetts. I had come twenty-three miles the day before and faced another seventeen to the next shelter, so it wasn't difficult to celebrate by doing nothing. I sat on the boat dock and "managed" the pond for the caretaker while she made a quick trip into a nearby town.

Turning fifty made me aware of how much unfinished business there was in my life. Even on the Trail, in an effort to be open and honest about my past, I had said things to reporters about my children that left them feeling hurt and exposed. Instead of mending the relationship with my kids, I had succeeded in widening the gap. Somehow, I needed to communicate an apology to them and let them know how much I loved them.

With my own siblings, I had work to do, too.

My sister, Midge, had visited me on the Trail a couple of days earlier, and we'd enjoyed a great time together. We were born eleven months apart and have always been close. But her visit stirred up a lot of unhappy memories for Midge. During our childhood, I had often taunted Midge in front of my friends. It took me years to realize how deeply she had been hurt by that.

Those things weighed me down so much that I had considered leaving the Trail until I could resolve them. But as I hiked and prayed, the Lord showed me that He was the only One who could make those things right. I prayed for the words to say to the people I had hurt and for the ability to trust the outcome to God.

Beyond the pressure of mending relationships with the people I loved, I felt the increasing pressure of the Trail.

The nights were already getting cooler, summer was nearing its end, and I still had 620 miles to go. If I was going to reach Katahdin by the middle of October, I would have to average ten miles per day for the rest of the hike, with no days off. That was a commendable goal, but probably not realistic. Many days I could hike twelve to fourteen miles, but the delays and time off conspired to keep my total under the necessary seventy miles a week.

Several hikers had flip-flopped to the northern end of the Trail and were now headed south. As autumn progressed, they would be heading toward warmer weather and had a better chance of not being stopped by snow. People had advised me several times to do the same, but I decided to keep heading north.

As I looked back on the years of my life, they seemed a lot like the Trail. Hiking began with a decision in the morning, followed by a lot of choices to keep going throughout the day. My inner healing seemed to follow a similar pattern. Hiking and healing happened one step at a time.

Ten miles was an insignificant part of two thousand, but if I strung together enough ten-mile days, I'd get from one end of the Trail to the other. Consistency and time were the keys. I had been walking God's trail for only two of my fifty years. My conversion experience was still fresh in my mind. There was still a long way to go, but I could say a big prayer of thanks every time I looked back at where I'd been.

When I finally crossed the border from Massachusetts into Vermont, the A.T. joined The Long Trail. For the next hundred miles, they would follow the same route until the A.T. veered eastward toward Hanover, New Hampshire, and The Long Trail continued north to Canada. When people asked what my next hike was going to be, I often joked, "The Long Trail, because I'll have a third of it already done."

I reached Manchester Center, Vermont, on August 25, and celebrated being three-fourths of the way to Katahdin. However, from what everyone told me, I still had seventy-five percent of the work left. After what we'd come through already, that was hard to believe. But people said that the last five hundred miles were the most physically taxing of any on the Trail.

On the positive side, a couple of hikers told me I could still finish without any trouble. They said October was the perfect month for outdoor sports in Maine.

Were they talking about hiking the A.T. or playing tennis in Bar Harbor?

It was hard to know who to believe.

The Trail in Vermont was strenuous, but enjoyable. The cooler days made hiking more pleasant, especially through the forests and across the old abandoned farmlands of the state. Each day brought the different smells of birch, hemlock, and several varieties of pine. I still had trouble getting on the Trail by ten o'clock in the morning, but the terrain allowed me to do some twelve-mile days before the sun dropped below the ridges.

In Vermont, I became almost certain of something I had suspected for a long time. Orient seemed to be following the white blazes on the trees. Because a dog's sight is his weakest sense and he looks mostly at ground level, I had never thought that Orient identified the blazes as Trail markings or followed them. But I was beginning to change my mind.

With the harness, I could tell when Orient was sniffing the ground or walking with his head up. When the A.T. abruptly changed direction or intersected another trail, Orient looked around before deciding which way to go. For the past fifteen hundred miles, the white blazes had been the most consistent aspect of the Trail. Knowing Orient, he had made the connection with the white blazes long before I gave him credit for it.

I stopped for a day in Hanover, New Hampshire, the home of Dartmouth College. A fellow hiker told me that all first-year students there are required to spend several days hiking in the mountains as part of their freshmen orientation. The famous Dartmouth Outing Club is a great supporter of the A.T. and maintains seventy-five miles of the Trail in New Hampshire and Vermont.

My fellow thru-hiker, Gary the Englishman, graciously drove me to the town of North Conway to get the clothing and supplies I needed for the next section of the hike. The White Mountains were waiting for me just over forty miles up the Trail. With a new tent and stove, and some better rain gear, I hoped to be prepared to face what many hikers called the ultimate challenge of the A.T.

Two days out of Hanover, I spent the night at the big Hexacuba Shelter. A Harvard student came in late that night and followed me onto the Trail the next morning, thinking we were going south. The first mile was a tough climb over a boulder field toward the summit of Mt. Cube. When I found out he was a southbounder, I tried to tell him he was going the wrong way. He didn't remember coming through the boulder field the night before and wasn't about to believe that he was wrong instead of me.

My grandmother used to describe a know-it-all as someone who "knew all four things." She would have described that confident but confused hiker as someone who "knew all four things and part of the fifth."

I understood how easy it was to get turned around, because I'd walked a mile and a half the wrong way out of a shelter a few days before. This time, however, I was confident about my direction and told him we were definitely headed north. I don't know if he finally believed me or whether he looked at his map, but he turned around and headed south.

Educating those Harvard guys was a tough job, but somebody had to do it.

Chapter Thirteen

Worst Weather in the World

Orient and I reached a road crossing about noon on the 12th of September. I thought it was probably New Hampshire Highway 25, but took out my audio cassette guide just to make sure. If the little village of Glencliffe was close enough, I planned to walk in and pick up a couple of items at the grocery store. I had been hiking in rain all morning but the sun was trying to peek through. A little sunshine and some candy bars might be all I needed to make it over Mt. Moosilauke before dark.

As I was listening to the tape, a man stopped and offered to drive me into town, which was only half a mile down the road. During our quick trip to the store and back to the Trail, he advised me to stop at Jeffers Brook, the next shelter, and postpone Mt. Moosilauke until the next day. It was seven and a half miles over the mountain, he said, and he thought I'd need a good night's rest and a full day to do it. He seemed to know what he was talking about, and his voice had a very insistent tone.

I didn't want to waste half a day, but I didn't want to do anything foolish either. Maybe Mt. Moosilauke was as tough as he said. On the other hand, it might turn out to be like most of the other places people had warned me about.

After six months on the Trail, I had decided that the most difficult part of the A.T. was the portion someone had just covered and was now describing to other hikers. "You've got the hardest part of the Trail right ahead," was a standard phrase.

People had warned me — with gruesome descriptions — of several trouble spots like Laurel Falls Gorge, Dragon's Tooth, Devils Racecourse, and the Lemon Squeezer.

In some places, hikers had left messages for me saying, "Bill, don't even attempt the next section. It's too difficult and dangerous for you." Most of the places were demanding, but by no means impossible. That's why I took all such warnings with a grain of salt.

But the direst warnings centered around the White Mountains in New Hampshire. Some said they would be the make-or-break point for my hike. Others said September was too late in the season to be able to avoid snow and bitter cold on the exposed ridges. A few people told me bluntly, "You'll never make it through the Whites."

Two-thirds of the A.T.'s 158 miles in New Hampshire wound through the White Mountains, crossing at least twenty-two peaks higher than four thousand feet. With the timberline at forty-two hundred feet, that meant hikers had a lot of exposure to the full fury of the elements. One section in the Presidential Range included thirteen continuous miles above the protection of the tree line.

The official Appalachian Trail Conference guidebook said: "The alpine ridge of the Presidential Range is exposed to storms that rise rapidly and are often violent, with hurricane-force winds and freezing conditions, even in summer. Carry ample extra clothing, and, if weather becomes threatening, promptly descend to shelter by the shortest route. If severe weather is predicted, take the shortcut which eliminates crossing the northern Presidential Range. Even this route can be forbidding in bad weather and should be approached cautiously."

I really didn't know how seriously to take these warnings. But I did know that it was mid-September and the first frost of autumn had just left my tent fly covered with a warning layer of white. The crunch of fallen leaves underfoot and the comments of hikers about the early signs of fall color should have quickened my pace, but they only seemed to add weight to my mental pack.

The nights didn't seem long enough to replenish the strength I expended each day. It was easier than ever to take time off, and increasingly difficult to force myself out of the sleeping bag to fix breakfast. It was a rare morning when I could manage to get packed up and on the Trail early.

Orient and I arrived at the Jeffers Brook Shelter about 1:00 p.m. With an afternoon alone, I could bring my taped journal up-to-date and dry everything in my pack that was still wet from the night before. I had covered only six miles that day over fairly level terrain, but I was worn out. This was a far cry from my seventeen-mile days in August, and I knew time was getting short. Maine's Baxter State Park officially closed for the winter on October 15. Even though hikers might be allowed to climb Katahdin after that date, there was a point at which snow and ice made the mountain impassable until spring.

Could I cover 390 miles *and* climb Katahdin in the next thirty days?

Orient and I took a leisurely stroll down to the brook and sat for a long time listening to it cascade into a huge pool just below a little waterfall. Sometime during the next couple of days, a writer from Colorado was supposed to meet me on the Trail and hike with me for a few days. I hoped he was a strong hiker and enjoyed mountains and macaroni, because that's all there would be for the rest of New Hampshire.

Not a soul came by during the two hours I spent there, thinking, praying, and soaking my feet in Jeffers Brook. When the sun began to drop toward the horizon, I filled my water bag and started back for the shelter. Orient hid in the trees and pounced on me as I walked back up the Trail.

He'd been very playful and it was good to see him feeling so frisky. I thought back to the hot days in Virginia when Orient would hide in the corner of the shelter every morning as I held his harness and pack. Every day, he seemed stronger and more eager to go.

A thru-hiker called Bearman arrived at the shelter just before dark. I had first met him way back in Georgia, then ran into him again in a shelter near Cheshire, Massachusetts. There he told me that he had run out of food and money, and wouldn't be able to complete his thru-hike without help. I felt the Lord wanted me to help him, so I began giving him some of the food my support group sent. Several other thru-hikers said he was a freeloader, but I figured we had met up for a reason.

Sometimes Bearman and I would hike together for several hours and stay at the same shelter. Then it might be two or three days before I ran into him again. We had several good talks about what it meant to surrender to the Lord, and I was hoping that he'd make some decisions that would stay with him after he finished the Trail.

Two other northbound thru-hikers, Island Time and Wunderboy, also spent the night with us at Jeffers Brook Shelter. They said that tomorrow, going over Mt. Moosilauke, we would climb four thousand feet in the first four miles, then descend three thousand feet on the other side to Beaver Brook Shelter. It would be our first climb above the tree line.

The next morning, I heard two men talking as they approached the shelter. One was a ranger named Ray, who had a food box for me. The other was Dave McCasland, the writer. The other guys admired Dave's new boots and kidded him about his T-shirt, which said, "Colorado — Don't Trust Anyone Under 14,000 Feet." I picked up his backpack and winced. It must have weighed seventy pounds.

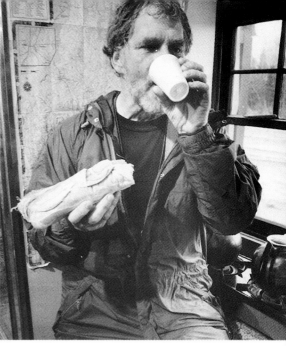

"Meeting people was my greatest pleasure on the Trail."
Credit: Bill Greene, Boston Globe

The average thru-hiker burns 6,000 calories a day.
Credit: Bill Greene, Boston Globe

One slip into Maine's icy waters could bring on hypothermia. "Orient's last step was my next step for 2,168 miles." *Credit: Bob DeLong, Bangor Daily News*

The Presidential Range of the White Mountains — thirteen continuous miles above treeline.
Credit: Bill Greene, Boston Globe

Relaxing on the back porch of The Inn, Hot Springs, NC. "I discovered that thru-hikers were a unique family and I was definitely part of it." *Credit: John Carter*

Trail Thing, Wordman, Hobbit, Rambling Dan and Butterfly Lady share a hot fire at Cold Spring Shelter, NC. "Names like that seemed normal on the A.T." *Credit: John Carter*

Irwin, Island Time (Kevin Rourke), Dave McCasland, and Wunderboy (Heath Clayton) on the summit of Mt. Moosilauke, NH. "Many people said I'd never make it through the White Mountains." *Credit: Heath Clayton, The Cary News.*

Rock cairns (upper left) mark the way through treeless boulder fields near Mt. Adams.
"Many times Orient had to go ahead and wait for me to catch up."
Credit: Bill Greene, Boston Globe

Bill and Orient catch forty winks in a warm cabin at Daicey Pond. "Orient is my constant companion, 24 hours a day." *Credit: Bill Greene, Boston Globe*

Wind-driven fog on Mt. Washington created arctic sculptures of rime ice. "September 24 — Arrived summit, 6 p.m. Wind 55 mph, temp. 27 degrees F. Wind chill, -10 degrees F." *Credit: Bill Greene, Boston Globe*

Orient was in charge of navigation, choosing the safest route for Bill. "The process is pretty simple. God leads Orient and Orient leads me." *Credit: Bill Greene, Boston Globe*

A clear alpine spring beckons Bill and Orient on a September afternoon. "After 8 1/2 months on the Trail, a drink of pure water is something I'll never take for granted again," *Credit: Bill Greene, Boston Globe*

Irwin receives a bear hug from friend, Bill Makepeace, at the end of the Trail. "Against all the odds, because of all the love and prayers, we made it." *Credit: Bill Greene, Boston Globe*

With winter threatening, Bill climbed Mt. Katahdin on October 24. "It was nice to have the mountain behind me, but I still had 190 miles to go." *Credit: Lynne Whelden*

Bill's family celebrated his A.T. victory and Thanksgiving at the Big Moose Inn. Back row, l-r: Jeff, Bill, Billy, Marianne Irwin Cash, Brooks Cash, Lynn Irwin (Bill's brother). Seated: Billy's wife, Cheryl, Bill's sister, Midge Irwin, Carolyn Starling, Lynn's wife Peggy, grandson Jonathan.

Bill's children, Marianne, Billy, and Jeff. "My kids were great encouragers from my first steps on the A.T. until the end."

Christmas, 1948. Bill's parents: Dr. Howard Irwin, Louise Irwin holding Lynn, Bill and Midge on floor.

Island Time, Wunderboy, and Bearman struck out at a fast pace and said they'd wait for us at the top. Dave walked behind me and I could tell he was struggling with his heavy pack. The climb up Moosilauke was rocky and steep, but certainly nothing I considered dangerous or unusually difficult. With a temperature in the low fifties it was ideal weather for hiking.

On the summit, Island Time and Wunderboy described the view while I loaded up on gorp, granola bars, and water. Dave took an aspirin and didn't say much. I told everyone that if this was what the White Mountains were all about, I thought they were a little overrated.

Once again, I had opened my mouth too soon.

On the north side of Moosilauke, the Trail went almost straight down. Each time Orient stopped, I used my ski pole to determine the angle of the rocks, the distance down to the next ledge, and the location of any trees or bushes I could grab for support. I released Orient and told him to go ahead while I climbed down from one small foothold to the next. He would jump down and wait, softly whining until I caught up with him. Several times a protruding branch snagged his pack or rocks wedged him tightly. Slowly, slowly, we made our way down in a light but steady drizzle.

Descending alongside the cascades of Beaver Brook, we encountered steep wooden steps anchored in grooves chiseled out of the smooth rock faces. They created a series of nearly perpendicular staircases with no handrail. Orient skidded on the first slippery step and began avoiding the others. He thought he was taking me the safest way, when actually just the opposite was true. I had to urge him to stay on the steps and off the glassy rocks. A thru-hiker had fallen here a few days before and sustained a serious head injury. I didn't want to be next.

Just as it got dark, we finally reached Beaver Brook Shelter, exhausted, but all in one piece. I felt duly welcomed to the Whites.

Other than avoiding the slick, wooden steps, Orient had done remarkably well coming over Moosilauke. Two days later, climbing South Kinsman Mountain, he met his match. The first time he stopped in front of a sheer rock face and sat whining, I was sure the Trail went around it. I felt with my stick but could find no other way.

I mumbled another complaint about the man who called this a "footpath," and gave Orient a boost. He whined when I pushed his haunches up over my head and I could hear his toenails scraping the rock as he scrambled up. I tossed my ski pole after him, then used both hands and feet to climb up. I wondered how in the world the people who built this Trail expected a blind man to negotiate these cliffs.

On one rock face, I ran out of energy and couldn't move. My fingers gripped a crevice above my head, but I didn't have the strength to pull myself up.

When my whole body began shaking, I knew I had to go up or let go and fall down to a certain injury.

Out loud, I asked God for strength.

Someone else must have been praying for me, too. I pulled again and within seconds was over the top.

During the ascent of Kinsman, I must have boosted Orient up over my head in at least twenty places. After a while, he was reluctant to scramble, and I was doing almost all the work. His toenails scraped and tore as he tried to climb.

We had been climbing into low, blowing clouds all morning. Just as we reached the exposed summit, a slashing rain hit us from behind. There were no warning drops, just the full force of icy water driven by a forty-mile-an-hour wind. Orient lost the Trail across the rocks, and Dave couldn't find it either. I was quickly soaked, with water running down my legs into my boots.

Just then, a voice behind called out, "The Trail's over here!" I said, "It must be an angel!"

It turned out to be Tim Post, a thru-hiker who had caught up with us just as we reached the summit. We followed him a quarter of a mile down into the protection of some trees, where we put on our rain jackets and pants. They would at least stop the chilling effect of the wind and capture some body heat, as long as we kept moving.

Covering only two miles during the entire morning had left me discouraged. The goal, Lonesome Lake Hut, was still four miles away, but once there we could spend a night inside, out of the weather. When we reached the shelter at Kinsman Pond in late afternoon, my feet were numb from the cold. The temperature had dropped to the 30s and a swirling mist chilled me to the bone. Another two miles from there to Lonesome Lake was out of the question.

All the tent sites at Kinsman were taken and the shelter was overflowing with weekenders, who graciously made room for us. They were having a great time, with all kinds of gourmet food and hot wine, but I couldn't imagine anyone hiking for fun in weather like that. Several hikers were gathered around a candle for a rousing game of "Cosmic Wimp-Out." It had something to do with three dice and the number ten, but I was too tired to try and figure it out.

The register was full of reactions to the rugged Trail and the weather. Van-Go's artistic entry from a few days earlier showed a hiker with suction-cup boots being held to the side of a vertical rock face. His caption read: "I love the Whites."

The highlight of the evening for me was meeting a southbounder named Steve. My friend, Lea Bolling of The Seeing Eye, had met him in Maine and told him to look for us. He played his guitar and sang "Amazing Grace" to a tune I had never heard before. After seven exhausting hours on the Trail, my spirit was lifted by Steve's singing.

The highlight for Orient was stretching out over the bottom of someone's warm sleeping bag. He was establishing himself as a real connoisseur of bags, and I think he identified the most expensive ones by smell and feel. Other thru-hikers had already discovered that, when they unrolled a bag in the shelter, they'd better be ready to climb in or Orient would beat them to it.

The next morning, as we hiked toward Lonesome Lake, Orient led me right over a large root that sent me sprawling. He'd had more than his share of "phooeys" from me during the past couple of days so I dropped his leash and gave him the command, "Fetch." Orient was supposed to pick up his leash in his mouth, walk around behind me, and stand on my left side until I took it from him. Then I could praise him and tell him what a good boy he was. He usually did it eagerly. But three times he spit the leash out as he walked behind me. I guess it was his way of saying he was too tired to do even the simplest thing right.

During the next several days, as Dave and I hiked together, our friendship deepened. I appreciated his willingness to walk behind us. When people hiked in front of Orient and tried to tell me where to go, it created problems. Dave followed several steps behind and said he'd talk when I wanted to, otherwise he'd be quiet. Sometimes we'd walk for an hour or two without saying a word. During our breaks, we laughed a lot, and I found it easy to tell him about the best and the worst parts of my life.

The daunting path the Trail took through the Whites was predictable, but the weather was not. One guidebook described it as "the worst weather in the continental United States," while the gift shop on Mt. Washington sold T-shirts boasting that the summit had "the worst weather in the world." The highest surface wind gust ever recorded, 231 mph, occurred there in 1934. One man told me that a mile and a half below the summit, an April wind in 1972 had lifted the entire roof off Lakes of the Clouds Hut and carried it into Amanoosuc Ravine, nine hundred yards away.

My journal recorded some weather notes that showed the erratic mood swings of the White Mountains:

Mon. 9/17 — Overnight at Liberty Spring Tent Site: 25 degrees, corn snow, frozen boots and water bag. Trail crew gave us a two-way radio so we could get weather reports and keep in touch. Radio weighs four pounds. Ugh!

Tues. 9/18 — Franconia Ridge/Mt. Lafayette: Snow, freezing fog/rime ice, wind gusts to 80 mph. Wind chill of -17 degrees F. Made five mi. to Greenleaf Hut.

Wed. 9/19 — Greenleaf Hut to Galehead Hut, 7.5 mi. Sunny, clear, in a.m., radio says visibility 100 mi. Arrived 8:00 p.m., just before pouring rain.

Thurs. 9/20 — Galehead Hut to Zealand Falls Hut, 6.5 mi., blowing rain, cold.

Fri. 9/21 — 60 degrees and sunny, Zealand Hut to Crawford Notch, 7.6 mi.

Mon. 9/24 — Cold, blowing mist. Helped dehydrated, hypothermic hiker on Mt. Eisenhower, used radio to call rescue team. Tea with Howard and Sue from New Zealand in "dungeon" at Lakes of the Clouds Hut. Arrived summit Mt. Washington, 6:00 p.m., wind 55 mph, temp. 27 degrees, wind chill -10 degrees F. Spent night in observatory with crew.

Tues. 9/25 — Mt. Washington: 6,288 feet. Second highest point on A.T. Clear, sunny, and cold. Wind 5 mph. Joined by Bill Greene, photographer from the Boston Globe.

One poetic hiker wrote, "The fog in the Whites doesn't tiptoe in on little cat feet. It tromps in wearing hobnail boots, pushed by the westerly winds of three converging storm tracks. It flies horizontally across the summits, leaving icy fingerprints on everything it touches."

I probably would have said, "Stand still in the Whites and you'll turn into a perspiration-flavored popsicle."

Hikers kidded a lot about the weather, but it was no joke. A plaque in the summit house on Mt. Washington recorded the names of 115 people who had died while hiking in the area. Most had been caught unprepared in sudden storms and perished from hypothermia and exposure.

But even with the volatile weather, my two hardest days came with sunshine and gentle breezes. I just wasn't ready for the seemingly endless array of rocks.

The trek from Mt. Washington to Madison Springs Hut was only six miles, and no one had said anything about the Trail being difficult. There was even a rumor that the A.T. went around two peaks instead of over them, and I found that too good to even hope for. I should have known there was a catch somewhere.

The catch was the simple fact that rough terrain, which was a minor inconvenience to other hikers, battered my feet and slowed me to a crawl. Boulder fields were the worst, and that's what lay in our path most of the way to Madison Hut. For mile after mile, there was no real trail, just painted blazes on rocks, and piles of stones called *cairns* to mark the way. Every step fell on an uneven and often unstable surface.

Most of the boulders on the Trail were small, the size of basketballs —and that was even worse on my legs and ankles. They were above ground and yet partially covered, so the ground itself was uneven and I was always twisting an ankle. And when there was no other way around a giant boulder, I had to push Orient up over my head and scramble up myself as best I could. This was no fun, particularly up above the tree line, where the wind was such a factor.

I complained a lot that day, mostly out of pain and frustration. Every step hurt and I must have fallen fifty times. The Trail signs conflicted with the distances in the Data Book and I thought we were closer to our destination than we actually were.

It was dark when we reached Thunderstorm Junction, where a sign said three-tenths of a mile to go. It took Orient and me nearly an hour and a half to descend the steep, rocky Trail. Madison Hut was closed for the season, so that night, three of us and Orient slept in a two-man tent.

Most nights, I took eight hundred milligrams of ibuprofen just to ease the pain from hiking. I called it Vitamin I. That night I took two and went to sleep in spite of the throbbing in my legs and feet.

The next day, I felt sure we could make the seven miles to Pinkham Notch, but once again the rocks prevailed.

Mt. Madison, another place no one ever mentioned as being difficult, created the worst single day for me thus far. From 9:30 a.m. to 5:00 p.m., I covered only three miles. Maybe I was tired from the day before, but I just couldn't move any faster or do any more. When we reached Osgood Tent Site, we were just over four miles from Pinkham Notch, but I was through for the day. We didn't make Pinkham until the next day.

During the next two days at Pinkham Notch, I must have spent three hours on the phone talking to Carolyn Starling, my children and close friends in North Carolina. Was I homesick? Maybe so. I knew I was tired of hiking, tired of being wet and cold, and tired of being away from the friends I hadn't seen in months.

It was the worst depression I'd known to that point on the Trail, and I think part of it was just sheer fatigue and the melancholy associated with fatigue. I thought *everything* was sad.

The other reason for my depression was the thought of leaving Pinkham. The Appalachian Mountain Club headquarters there has everything to make you comfortable, including a dining hall where you can eat all you want. There is a welcoming lodge, educational programs for the public, a motel that can sleep a couple of hundred people, and a wonderful store that sells much-needed supplies.

I could have stayed there the rest of my life! I really should have stayed only one night, but I stayed two, and was looking for a reason to stay a third. Each time I'd hear through the grapevine that another friend was coming up the A.T., I delayed. There were ten to twenty people I knew there every single day — and *none* of us wanted to leave!

Not only that but, once you leave, you're faced with a steep, notoriously hard climb up Wildcat Mountain. Of course, anytime you left a town in that area, you almost always faced a really steep climb. After all, most towns are in gaps, not on mountaintops. And when you're leaving a town you always re-supply, so you always have your heaviest pack going up another steep grade. Everybody dreaded leaving Pinkham, especially when the weather was bad. Which was always.

For me, there was an added sadness because Dave left from Pinkham Notch to head home. The four-day hike he had planned had turned into two weeks on seventy-five miles of the roughest terrain on the A.T. He'd been a big encouragement and help during some rough days on the Trail.

As we stood near the highway, waiting for his bus to Boston, he said, "Bill, I can't say this hasn't been fun, because it hasn't." We laughed and promised to meet again in Maine for the last leg of the Trail through the Hundred Mile Wilderness.

All of these circumstances were making me sad. I sat for hours by the fire fantasizing about being home with friends, sitting in my hot tub.

I tried to stay busy doing inconsequential things, accepting meal invitations from friends, hoping to stretch my stay out to two weeks.

Another thing that kept me from really pushing it was that people kept telling me that, even if I didn't hike another mile, I was already a winner. A few said, "You've done more than most thru-hikers and come farther than anyone thought possible. If you end the hike now, no one could accuse you of not giving it everything you have."

If I needed a good reason to quit, they were making it easy.

On the other hand, I knew that refusing to face reality would be foolish. When a lady asked, "How will you feel if you don't make it to Katahdin?" I told her I'd just have to accept whatever the Lord enabled me to do. If He wanted me to make it, I would. If He didn't, I'd have to believe that was His will. To some people, putting the outcome of my hike in God's hands probably sounded like a cop-out. But it was the only way I knew to approach it.

I finally left Pinkham Notch. The Carter-Moriah Range from Pinkham Notch to Rattle River Shelter was more difficult than anyone had predicted, but I was getting used to that. There probably weren't any easy days between my current location and Katahdin. The sooner I quit wishing for one, the better off I'd be.

As I trudged towards the Rattle River Shelter, I thought of all the new friends I'd made in New Hampshire and was thankful for what each one meant to me. Along the Trail, hundreds of people had helped us on our way. I still believed they were God's angels and, without every one of their unselfish acts of kindness, I wouldn't have made it through each day.

On a Wednesday afternoon, Orient and I reached the junction of the A.T. and U.S. Highway 2, a few miles outside of Gorham, New Hampshire. We had made it through the Whites, in spite of all the grave predictions against it.

It was October 3 and we had come eighteen hundred miles.

But Katahdin waited nearly three hundred miles ahead, and Baxter State Park officially closed in twelve days.

Chapter Fourteen

Rain, Rocks, and Roots

The Trail in Maine is not user-friendly.

Orient and I entered steep mountains in the western part of the state and faced seven, four thousand-foot peaks with nine others above three thousand feet. Between the summits, the rise and fall in elevation was disheartening. In the seven miles from Old Speck Mountain to the top of Baldpate, the Trail took us down twenty-three hundred feet and back up another two thousand feet.

After the mountains, there would be another 170 miles of ponds and bogs before Katahdin.

The good news was that, by October, most of the insects, including the ruthless black flies, were gone. The bad news was that the days were getting shorter and Indian summer would be only a temporary guest.

Other than Mt. Katahdin, Mahoosuc Notch was the last of the obstacles people said would be impossible for Orient and me. The Notch was a massive, mile-long boulder field littered with rocks as big as automobiles. Pictures and descriptions of it appeared in almost every book about the A.T., and it was definitely one of those "Wait till you get here" places.

Several hikers had told me about their journey through Mahoosuc Notch and it sounded tough. They spoke of crawling under rocks and removing their packs so they could squeeze through narrow passageways. One girl said she got so frustrated that she sat down, cried, and had what she called "a deep-woods crisis" right there on a rock.

The more I heard people talk, the more it seemed that lack of time was often a bigger problem than the physical difficulties. Hikers who were used to doing high-mileage days were angered by one mile that required two hours of their time. I decided to devote an entire day to Mahoosuc Notch and try to have fun. My decision was made a lot easier by four new friends from Massachusetts who joined me.

Alice, Jim, Helen and Mike met me at Gentian Pond campsite near the Maine/New Hampshire state line. Alice was a freelance writer who had tried to set up a meeting with me for months. When we met, she and her friends brought along yet another new pair of custom-made boots I'd ordered. These companions hiked with me periodically from then on.

On Sunday, October 7, we started through Mahoosuc Notch, and all the prophets of doom and gloom must have been disappointed. The temperature was in the high sixties and the rocks radiated warmth from a bright sun. I let Orient go ahead so he could scramble from one boulder to another and find his own way through. I needed both hands for stability, so holding his harness was out of the question until we reached the other side.

I had begun the day by taking a headfirst fall on the Trail down from Goose Eye Shelter. Jim and Mike carried my pack, leaving me free to concentrate on staying in one piece. It would have been much more difficult to negotiate with that burden on my back. With the whole day to make the two miles from the shelter through the Notch, we were able to relax and have a good time together. Halfway through we stopped for a bite of lunch, then stretched out for a nap. I felt like I was somewhere on the beach sunbathing. Who would have predicted that October in Maine could be so warm?

Orient had more difficulty than anyone, even though Helen carried his pack. He became wedged several times in crevices and had to wait for me to catch up and help him out. He tore a couple of toenails scrambling on the rocks, and was limping slightly by the time we made it through.

I camped on a nice level spot half a mile beyond the Notch. Jim and Mike told me that the area around my tent site looked like a fantasy world of golden leaves. The deciduous trees were at their peak of color and I tried to picture the scene in my mind. My friends left with the promise that we'd meet again. Orient and I hustled inside the tent just as it began to rain.

The next day, Orient and I broke camp in the rain and hauled ourselves up Mahoosuc Arm, a fifteen hundred-foot vertical rise in just two miles. We reached Speck Pond Shelter atop Old Speck Mountain by early afternoon. Orient was limping, and I needed to dry out. My eight-mile goal for the day faded to three, and we climbed into the shelter, grateful for what we had been able to do.

I did a lot of thinking and praying that day about the people God had brought into my life through the hike. It didn't matter that I didn't know what they looked like. I knew their voices, their personalities and their kind ways.

Deep inside, I had a peace about where I was on the Trail.

While the A.T. in Maine was rough and unyielding, the people couldn't have been more friendly. Growing up in the South, I had always heard that the farther north you went, the more unfriendly the people became. If you ever got as far north as Maine, heaven forbid, you'd be lucky to find anyone who would even say hello. Maybe that was a holdover from the Civil War. After all, these people up here had a magazine called "Yankee" and they were actually proud of it. I was a Southern boy, but I fell in love with every Mainer I met.

One of the first things they did was teach me how to talk. I had my "Rs" and "ahs" all mixed up. I had to learn to ask for pizzer, soders and candy bahs. My friend Art became Aht, the battery in my headlamp was a battry, and everybody in the state was a Maine-ah. The mountain I was heading for was pronounced Katardin, not Katahdin. It was going to take a little time, but I was willing to learn.

I discovered that the people in Maine loved their state and weren't very interested in leaving. On Interstate 95, the last barrier between Maine and New Hampshire is the Kittery Bridge over the Piscataqua River. No "Maine-ah" ever wanted to go "fa'tha" than the "Kitry" Bridge. Lucky for them that I, a Southerner, didn't talk funny, too.

In Andover, Pat and Larry Wyman gave me a royal welcome at their bed and breakfast. There, Ron Theriault joined me to hike through the rugged Bemis Range. Back at Pinkham Notch, Carolyn had relayed a message that Ron wanted to hike with me for a while.

Ron was a hiker who was familiar with the rough terrain here, and that would be a big help to me physically. In return, I could counsel with him along the way. It went well; we both seemed to benefit from the time together.

The second night out, Ron and I realized there had been a Trail relocation and we were a lot farther from Bemis Mountain Shelter than we had thought. At 6:30 p.m., in the swirling snow, I put on a headlamp so Orient could see, and Ron switched on his flashlight. Within an hour, I was exhausted and I told Ron I couldn't take another step. The only thing I knew to do was pray, so I just talked to the Lord about our situation: "Lord, You know where we are and why we're here." I said. "We're out doing Your work, so please give us the energy to get to the shelter, or show us a place where we can camp."

Within a few minutes, my legs had stopped aching and I was able to pick up my pace. Even Orient seemed more nimble and alert. By nine o'clock, I was wondering if we had somehow passed the shelter, when Ron saw a sign saying it was only one hundred yards away. We both shed some tears of joy and relief.

My only explanation for what happened that night, and many other times on the Trail, is that God gave Orient and me the strength we needed. I know some people would chalk it up to positive thinking or drawing on some kind of deep inner strength, but I'm convinced that God answered my prayers.

Ron was a great encouragement and, when we parted, he told me that a lot of people in Rumford would be praying for us all the way to Katahdin. That was what Orient and I needed most. I had never encountered anything like the A.T. It took me to the very edge of physical and mental exhaustion almost every day. No matter how much strength I had in the morning, it was completely gone before I reached that day's destination.

I guess the Lord put me on the Trail with my blindness to let other people see what He could do. My job was to show up for work every day and walk as far as He gave me strength to walk. God needed a weak man for that job, somebody who had to depend on Him for every step. Some people feel that the Apostle Paul's "thorn in the flesh" was failing eyesight. A few scholars think that, later in his life, he may have been almost blind. No one knows for sure what it was, but he walked a lot of miles with that "thorn."

Maybe it was that his toenails had fallen off, just like mine.

When Phil Pepin met Orient and me near Rangeley, I felt like we were getting a guided tour of the A.T. in Maine. Phil was a two-time thru-hiker who lived in Stratton and knew the country around there the way I knew the streets of Burlington. His work on the Maine Appalachian Trail

Executive Committee gave him a feel for the A.T. that few other people had.

I appreciated every ounce of help offered to Orient and me, and sensed that those who helped were doing it because they wanted to, not because they felt some kind of obligation. Phil was very generous with his time and with his home, which became our headquarters for nearly ten days. After hiking a portion of the Trail in rain or snow, it was great to return to a warm bed and a good meal each night.

One of our first days out, Hurricane Lili threw her final punch at New England before spiraling out into the North Atlantic. All around us, trees were being toppled by the fierce winds. They sounded like giant firecrackers as their trunks snapped and they crashed to the forest floor. I knew Phil was worried, but I figured that, even if I could see, I probably wouldn't have time to avoid a falling tree. Besides, the Lord was in charge of the wind and our safety. Nothing was going to happen to us that wasn't supposed to happen.

Fallen trees known as "blowdowns" confront hikers all along the A.T., but that day I knew why there were so many across the Trail in Maine. In a single day, thousands of trees would fall in the densely forested areas all across the state. Scores would lie across the A.T., forcing hikers to skirt them or break through the limbs. The Maine Appalachian Trail Club (MATC) sent crews out regularly to clear the Trail, but there was no way they could keep up with the storms.

A few days later, we hiked the Saddleback Range and Spaulding Mountain in freezing rain and snow. Phil told me that, once winter arrived, it was usually there to stay. Baxter State Park was officially closed, but the officials said they would do everything in their power to allow me to climb Katahdin when I arrived. But all of us knew that the weather wasn't in their power.

It was about this time that Carolyn Starling probably got more frustrated with me than at any other time on the whole trip. From around Harper's Ferry on, everybody was telling me that I needed to flip-flop the A.T. — that I needed to go to Katahdin and work my way back down. But the only way to get to me was to call Carolyn and ask *her* to give me the sales pitch. As more people called her and presented their case, she, too, became convinced that I needed to flip-flop.

Of course, I disagreed with her. I was convinced my instructions came from God and He hadn't given me any indication I should do it. Carolyn would then list the arguments she'd been given. These built up continuously, and got worse from Harper's Ferry on.

The height of Carolyn's frustrations came when Buzz Caverly, the director of Baxter State Park, called her as I started getting close to Stratton, Maine.

He said, "If Bill doesn't do Katahdin now, he won't be allowed to complete the hike later."

Carolyn agreed to pass on his message, but said she had to soften Buzz's strong words. She knew by now that when somebody treats me that way, trying to force me to do something with real strong words, it elicits an impenetrable brick wall from me. So she repeated Buzz's message, but softened the blow somewhat. It was still pretty direct.

I said, "I'll pray about it."

Carolyn said, "Bill, prayer is wonderful, but now is the time to listen to the people who care about you!"

I could feel the frustration boiling inside her, but I had to know for sure that's what I was supposed to do.

Finally, on October 20, with Carolyn's help, Buzz called me at Phil's and asked if he could drive down and talk with me. I told him I could guess what he wanted to talk about and thought we could cover it on the phone.

He told me he wanted me to climb Katahdin in the next few days.

At Carolyn's suggestion, he softened his words somewhat. But, in the end, Buzz shot straight with me: Katahdin was 184 Trail miles northeast of Stratton, and the weather was already getting rough on the mountain. As much as he wanted to help me complete the hike, his first responsibility was the safety of everyone using the park. If there was ice on Katahdin when I arrived, he would have to deny me entrance to the park. Would I consider driving to Baxter and climbing the mountain now?

I told Buzz I'd pray about it. A lot of hikers did it and it certainly wasn't against any thru-hiking ethic.

So I talked to the Lord about it and consulted a couple of close friends. There were a lot of things going through my mind as I struggled with the decision. Did I believe that the Lord could control the weather and keep the mountain clear for a few more weeks? Was it testing God to keep hiking and expect Him to hold off winter just for me? Would it be foolish to ignore the strong recommendation of a man who had spent thirty years in Baxter State Park?

I became convinced it was time to climb Katahdin for the safety of everyone concerned, but to do it without any prior publicity.

I think Buzz was relieved and, frankly, so was I. Several newspaper and television reporters had been asking when I would finally reach Katahdin. Several of them had planned to climb the mountain with me. One TV producer wanted to hire a helicopter to drop his camera crew on the top. If a lot of inexperienced people with heavy equipment went up the mountain, someone was bound to get hurt.

I had also wanted to be alone with the Lord for a few minutes at the top of Katahdin. A swarm of photographers might have prevented that or turned it into something I didn't want. Many of the reporters covering the hike had become friends, so I hoped they'd be able to understand my decision.

Buzz assured me he could keep the secret and would close the park to everyone but me on the appointed day. I asked Phil Pepin to climb with me, along with Lynne Whelden, my filmmaker friend from Pennsylvania. Buzz said he'd figure out a way to answer questions without lying for a couple of days, and the plans were made for an October 24 ascent.

I was in and out of Phil Pepin's house for a couple of days until the morning came when he drove us to Katahdin in his pickup truck — about a four-hour drive.

In some ways, climbing Katahdin would be an anti-climax to something I had anticipated for months. I had started talking about Katahdin with my first step off Springer Mountain. For a long time, it had seemed a remote, unattainable goal. Yet being able to stand at the top, kiss the sign, and raise my arms in victory was a vision I shared with every other thru-hiker. We looked forward to it as the crowning physical and emotional experience of the A.T.

Climbing Katahdin out of sequence would be different than I had imagined, but probably more like it should be. The big moments of my life had rarely lived up to the expectations I had heaped on them. This reminded me that the journey, not the destination, was the important thing.

My real objective had never been mountains, but people. When fellow hikers "oohed" and "aahed" over the view from each new summit, I was content with another vision. Katahdin was always part of the plan, but it would never be the ultimate achievement.

Chapter Fifteen

Katahdin

The Indians feared Mt. Katahdin and believed it was the home of an evil spirit called *Pamola*, who didn't like anyone climbing up to his house. The Indians said he captured people and took them under the mountain for a little "re-education program." For three hundred years, stories had been told of Indians, hunters, and soldiers who disappeared on Katahdin and were never seen again. Modern hikers who waited out storms in their tents at Daicey Pond — at the foot of the mountain — spoke of postponing their ascent until Pamola cleared the peak.

I wasn't worried about Pamola, but I had a lot of respect for the mountain.

Buzz Caverly said that, whenever people showed up from Boston in the latest high-fashion hiking clothes, saying they were ready to conquer Katahdin, he knew they weren't carrying a full string of fish. The mountain could be climbed, but never conquered.

In thirty years as a park ranger, Buzz had seen just about everything. He had arrested one noted thru-hiker three times for trying to climb Katahdin before the park opened in May. One summer, Buzz had climbed Katahdin twenty-three times, eighteen of them at night, usually to rescue exhausted or injured hikers. His worst times involved retrieving the bodies of people whose failure to read the signs and use sound judgment had cost them their lives. His voice still cracked when he told me about carrying the body of a thirteen-year-old boy off the mountain.

He was concerned with my safety and I was thankful for all his efforts, even though I jokingly referred to him as Buzz (Don't Die In My Park) Caverly. As far as I was concerned, his word was the law. Buzz had done everything he could to make it a safe, successful ascent.

Unfortunately, even he couldn't stop the rain.

We spent the night of October 23 at Daicey Pond Campground. The wood stove quickly warmed our little cabin and I was thankful to be indoors instead of tented out in the downpour. I fell asleep listening to the rain drum against the windowpane, hoping the dawn would bring sun.

The next morning, it was still raining as we made the short drive to Katahdin Stream Campground. At 7:30 a.m., we started to climb. Here, the A.T. followed the Hunt Trail for 5.2 miles, with a vertical ascent of four thousand feet to the mile-high summit of Katahdin. Phil led the way while Lynne tried to position himself for pictures. Orient and I brought up the rear. Heavy rain continued and, in many places, the Trail was a running stream.

Orient scrambled up and around the rocks, while I used as handholds the metal bars placed along parts of the route. The weather was miserable, but not bitter cold, considering the elevation and the exposure.

I felt sorry for Lynne, because his video camera was malfunctioning in spite of all his efforts to keep it warm and dry. I was more concerned about him than his camera, because he was wearing jeans and was soaked from the waist down. In the chilling wind, he was a prime candidate for hypothermia.

Phil and I carried our packs with a tent, sleeping bags, a stove and food. Winter survival gear was required for any ascent of Katahdin in threatening weather.

We covered the four miles to Thoreau Spring in four hours, and pressed ahead to the summit.

Once at the top, I posed by the sign for a picture, then found a quiet minute to pray. The weather encouraged a quick prayer. In the same breath with "Amen," I said, "It's cold up here. Let's get down off this thing."

I probably could have been more profound, but it was really getting cold. We were all spending a lot of energy just keeping the use of our hands. Lynne had already lost the use of his, and had had to turn back as soon as we reached the summit. The end result of all this activity — the pouring rain, the hypothermic weather, the fact that it was 2:00 p.m., and we still had 3.8 miles to go to get down — meant there wasn't much mental or physical energy left to think or to do something significant. I had little time to reflect. It was great to reach the summit, but we still had a steep four miles down before I could even think of being relieved.

The emotional euphoria I had expected just wasn't there, either. If it had been the end of the hike and a beautiful sunny day, it might have been different, but I'm not sure. I just remember being disappointed that I wasn't any more pleased with the accomplishment than I was.

The hike was far from over and the feeling of completion was still somewhere ahead.

We had hoped to be down the mountain by late afternoon, but our 5:00 p.m. radio check with Buzz told him we were still hours away. He started up the Trail to meet us, accompanied by a thru-hiker called Youngblood. A sighted hiker might have been able to scramble down the loose gravel and over the slippery ledges of the Abol Trail, which we had chosen for our descent. But Orient and I could only creep along, trying to make sure each step wouldn't send us tumbling. In some places, the water on the Trail was nearly up to my knees.

Phil was trying to talk me down, describing the Trail and giving advice on where to step and what to hold. I knew he wanted to help me, but by seven o'clock, my mind was on overload from voices telling me what to do. I told him I appreciated everything he had done for me, but I just couldn't listen to him any more. I asked him to go on ahead and let Orient and me work it out on our own.

I began to pray for peace of mind so that I could complete the 3.8 miles to the bottom.

Taking the Abol Trail back down had been a terrible mistake. The Trail was so steep and so treacherous that, with what felt like an eighty-percent grade, it was literally a gravel slide. In the rain and cold, every step was dangerous.

Katahdin was certainly on my Top Ten list of difficult places as it combined physical challenges in a unique way on the A.T. Going up, the huge boulders reminded me of Mahoosuc Notch, while coming down, the loose gravel made me feel I was walking down a steep bank of styrofoam peanuts. There was no secure footing anywhere, and my best attempts to step lightly often sent me into an uncontrolled slide.

It was 9:30 p.m. by the time we finally got down off the mountain. Buzz had brought sandwiches, hot tea, and confirmation of what I had suspected all day — three inches of rain had fallen during the past twenty-four hours.

Katahdin was behind me. With less than two hundred miles left to go, my finish line was now at the bottom of "the greatest mountain," not the top. It wasn't the end and the end wasn't in sight, so there was no real sense of accomplishment.

But we had made it, and that counted for something.

The next day, we sent out a press release telling our friends in the media what I had done and why. Buzz graciously allowed me to invite all of them to come to Baxter State Park and walk the last 2.4 miles with Orient and me on the final day of the hike. It would mean a lot of extra work for him and his staff, but they seemed genuinely happy to do it. Buzz responded to every impossible task with his standard reply, "Small job."

The afternoon before, Buzz had spent a lot of time on the phone fending off several members of the press who had somehow caught wind of my early ascent of Katahdin. After one TV producer received the press release, he called Buzz and accused him of lying, deliberate deception, and all manner of other heinous crimes.

The next day, back in Stratton, I received a call from the same man, more angry than ever about not being able to cover my ascent of Katahdin. I understood how he felt because that was his job and he had a reputation for doing it well. I just told him that, before he crawled in bed that night, he should get down on his knees and thank God that he and his crew hadn't been on the mountain with us.

Unfortunately, there had been one casualty during my ascent — Luanna, my talking watch. She drowned. The last time I heard her announce the time, she gurgled something about nine o'clock, and that was it. Bless her little digital heart.

I was ready to get back on the Trail and head north. Orient's coat was getting thick and he was awake every morning at five, giving everyone within reach a lick in the face and a cold nose in the ear. He wouldn't listen when I tried to cancel the daily wake-up call.

I thought back to the hot, humid days in Virginia when he would hide in the corner of the shelter every morning, hoping I wouldn't put on his harness and ask him the usual question, "Do you want to go for a little walk?" (It had gotten to be a standard thru-hiker joke.) The Trail had been a drudgery for Orient then. Now, the outdoors had become his life, and he seemed to thrive on the challenge of each new day.

I still couldn't set a date for ending this trek, but it was beginning to look more and more like Thanksgiving. Could I cook a turkey with a camping stove?

Chapter Sixteen

Time Alone

Just before Orient and I left Stratton for the last time on Sunday, October 28, Phil Pepin gave me a key to the fire warden's cabin on top of Bigelow Mountain. If the weather was bad, he said, I could stay there instead of in the shelter. Phil had already done so much for me I could never adequately thank him. These Maine-ahs just kept on giving.

We hugged each other and it was hard for me to leave, even though I was eager to head north. I just *had* to make good mileage every day from now on. This was Maine, and people kept saying that Lady Winter was standing in the wings, just waiting for her cue to take center stage.

Hunting season had begun, so Orient wore a bright orange bandana around his neck and I had a fluorescent vest draped over my pack. The big news story in Maine was the trial of a hunter who had killed a lady the year before. She was in her backyard wearing white gloves, and he mistook her for a deer.

The rain at the base of Bigelow Mountain soon turned to snow and continued throughout our seven-and-a-half mile climb over South Horn and West Peak. The A.T. led us right to the Avery Memorial Lean-to, but the temperature was dropping and I knew it was important to try and locate the fire warden's cabin. The elevation here was almost four thousand feet, and a three-sided shelter would be like a deep-freeze during the night. I left my pack in the lean-to and took Orient out to do some scouting around.

After finding the cabin, we had a difficult time retracing our steps to the lean-to. Then, we were unable to find our way directly back to the cabin. They were only one hundred yards apart, but the ankle-deep snow and sagging tree limbs blocking the Trail disoriented both me and Orient. I was greatly relieved when we finally found the cabin again and got inside.

I used the cabin's gas stove to boil some water for supper, and filled a hot-water bottle to put in my sleeping bag and warm my frozen feet. There was a wood stove for heat, and a small supply of split firewood inside the cabin. It was a great place to be for the night, and I fell asleep mumbling prayers of thanks for a lot of people and blessings the Lord had sent my way.

The next morning, I found about four inches of snow on the cabin porch, and knew that the steep climb up and down Avery Peak was going to be treacherous. We would just have to take it slowly. The next lean-to was six and a half miles away, but two thousand feet lower than the cabin. Surely the snow depth would diminish as we traveled down the mountain.

I put Orient's harness and pack on him, shouldered my own load and locked the cabin door behind me. When I stepped off the porch, I was up to my knees in snow. Thinking it was a drift, I kept walking, and was soon up to my hips. Orient couldn't walk at all. He jumped from one place to the next and sank up to his shoulders every time. There was no way he could travel like that.

A short walk behind the cabin revealed the same depth there, so we went back inside, built a fire, and I asked the Lord what we should do. The answer, at least for that day, seemed to be, "Stay put."

I gathered snow to melt for water and used the wood sparingly to keep some heat in the cabin.

Unfortunately, I had returned Phil's two-way radio before leaving Stratton, so I was without a way to let people know I was okay. The weather report from a little transistor radio in the cabin mentioned only one to three inches of snow in the higher elevations, and predicted a warming trend. Maybe the sun would melt things enough for me to leave the next day. I had enough food for Orient and myself for a couple of days, so I planned to be up and out of there early in the morning.

Tuesday morning was clear and sunny, but freezing cold. The snow around the cabin hadn't melted at all. I listened to my cassette Trail guide and thought about leaving, but became convinced it was a foolish thing to do. The cabin was in a *col,* or gap, between West Peak and Avery Peak. It was four-tenths of a mile from the cabin to the top of Avery Peak, and then a precipitous descent dropped two thousand feet in less than a mile.

I remembered one hiker's story of suffering frostbitten feet because he kept thinking it would get better.

I decided to stay another day.

Orient and I went exploring and located the lean-to again. There was supposed to be a spring nearby, but we couldn't find a sign or a trail. We'd have to keep melting snow for water. Phil had told me there was a fully stocked woodshed not far from the cabin. Since the wood supply in the cabin was getting very low, we spent a couple of hours searching for the shed, but it remained hidden. The location of the privy was also a mystery. I figured the caretaker in charge of the area would forgive me for using the woods.

The afternoon temperature must have been in the fifties but there was so much snow, it would be days before it melted enough for us to hike. Outside of our beaten paths, the snow was still knee-deep for me and a constant struggle for Orient.

I knew the Lord was in charge of this situation, but it didn't make any sense. Why was I stranded in a cabin on top of a mountain when I could have been making good time on the Trail just a few thousand feet lower? The radio announcer was talking about Indian summer in Augusta and Bangor. Up here, the overnight low would probably be in the twenties.

About three o'clock, a plane flew over so low I thought it was going to hit the trees. I tied an orange bandana to my ski pole and hustled outside, but it never came back over. Maybe no one had reported us missing.

I swept the cabin out twice, hung the rugs out to dry on the porch, made popcorn, and had supper ready by 4:30 in the afternoon. Without Luanna, I had to rely on brief radio checks for the time. Orient was content to sleep when we weren't out exploring, but my mind kept churning with all the possibilities, wondering what I should do.

That night, I began rationing the last of the wood, burning one stick at a time and adding another only onto glowing coals. I was a little drowsy, so I lay by the stove in my sleeping bag, thinking and praying.

It seemed as if I'd spent an awful lot of time alone during my life, much of it as a child at home. People in Leeds probably thought we were the ideal family, but there was a lot of emotional distance, especially between my father and me. In some ways, we had always been strangers.

When I was ten months old, Dad had gone into the service just before World War II. He may have come home twice between then and the time I was seven years old. My mother raised my sister, Midge, and me until the day a strange man called Dad showed up at our house and stayed.

He became a very skilled general surgeon whose ability to treat burns and do skin grafts drew people from all over the South. In our town, most people ranked him right up there with God. I knew he was a good doctor, but I lived in constant fear of his disapproval and rage.

When I was fifteen, Dad had one of his violent outbursts of temper at the breakfast table and struck me in the face. A few days later, two older friends and I left Leeds in an old Mercury, with three dollars between us. We got as far as Tuscaloosa, Alabama, where we worked for enough gas money to get us to Texas.

When we got there, my uncle in Rockwall said I could live with him and work in his bakery for a few weeks, until a job in the oil fields opened up. I got so sick of donuts when I worked there that it was thirty years before I ate another one. It wasn't high adventure, but I didn't have to live in fear of my father, either.

Even though I was only fifteen, I was fully grown and looked a lot older. When an offer came to join a roughneck crew, I fried my last donut and headed one hundred miles southeast to Jacksonville, between Tyler and Palestine, Texas.

My friends from Alabama left after two weeks on the drilling rig, but I stayed on. We worked seventy hours a week at two dollars per hour, plus overtime. That was good money for a kid in 1955.

Before long, I found a girlfriend. Of course, it wasn't long before we were having the same kind of arguments we used to have with our parents. Whatever I had fled from at home had followed me into the relationship I thought would solve everything.

As a teenager, I had been able to see the destructive patterns in my father and mother, but was blind to the beginnings of identical patterns in my own life.

After six months as a roughneck, I returned to Leeds with my own car and a determination that things would be different. I went back to high school and agreed to pay room and board at home in exchange for no curfew, no rules, and no parental control. Before I graduated from high school, I married for the first time.

The oil fields taught me a lot about life, but left me scarred morally and physically. I would never forget trying to stand close enough to a fire to warm my throbbing feet after working in icy water for an entire day. Since then, the smell of wood smoke has often flashed that scene into my mind.

I was trying to get close, trying to get warm; my feet were so cold I was crying, and wisps of smoke stung my eyes and my nose.

Need to get closer to the fire... closer to someone... wood smoke... feet hurt so bad... still alone...

I woke with a start and realized I was crying but didn't know why. Maybe it was the smoke curling out of the stove, or the fact that my feet were throbbing. Could it be Mother and Dad, both dead, but still remembered with a mixture of longing and regret? Maybe it was just being alone.

As I laid my last stick of firewood on the coals, an old hymn came to mind: "When upon life's billows you are tempest tossed; when you are discouraged thinking all is lost; Count your many blessings, name them one by one, and it will surprise you what the Lord has done."

Since there was no one to disturb but Orient, I started thanking God out loud for everything, including the snow that had forced me to stay in that cabin. It was a long thank-you list that included a lot of people and my present situation. Even though the wood was gone and Orient was out of food, I thanked God that He was still in charge. That was enough to sleep on.

The next morning, I shared my oatmeal with Orient and mixed him a big bowl of instant milk. It wasn't the best nourishment in the world for a German Shepherd, but it was better than nothing. About mid-morning we slowly began walking the edge of the woodline around the cabin, looking for the woodshed.

At one point, Orient ducked under some snow-laden limbs and pulled hard on the leash. I shook the snow off the limbs and followed him down a short trail... right to the woodshed. I hollered, "Praise God!" and carried an armful back to the cabin.

Still determined to find the spring, we walked down to the lean-to in the afternoon and tried to break a trail through the snow in the direction indicated by a sign.

I was one hundred yards down from the shelter when someone said, "Boy, am I glad to see you!"

I thought I was hearing things, so I just kept walking. When the voice spoke again. I said, "Who are you?" It was Peter Martel (Mr. Moleskin), with Art Batchelder (AB Positive) right behind. If Orient hadn't started licking their hands, I probably would have.

Moleskin hiked five miles back down the mountain to tell everyone I was safe. Art spent the night and we hiked down the next morning with Phil Pepin, who arrived early to make sure things were okay.

As we reconstructed it later, my friends Alice and Helen had been coming from the north, and we were supposed to meet at the Little Bigelow Lean-to on Monday night. But when everyone else met there except me, they figured I must be somewhere between Stratton and the lean-to, namely the fire warden's cabin — and that's when AB Positive and Mr. Moleskin decided to go looking for me.

The two men left Wednesday morning in the still-deep snow, and it took them nearly six hours to go the three miles to the cabin. Afterwards, we all retired to Phil's house.

Friday morning I was back on the Trail.

I still didn't understand why the Lord had put me in that cabin alone for three days. Maybe it was to remind me that He was in charge and the hike was still on His schedule, not mine. I know the Lord wanted to keep me humble and thankful for all I had. He may have wanted to remind me of everything I could do without.

Chapter Seventeen

So Close, Yet So Far

Most of the loons had left Pierce Pond by the time I arrived on Saturday, November 3. A couple of them called in the distance during the night, undoubtedly making their plans to leave soon for a warmer climate. That should have been my cue to head south, too, but Orient and I still had 150 northbound miles to go. The end of the Trail seemed so close, yet so far.

Dave McCasland came back from Colorado and met me at Pierce Pond Shelter to hike the rest of the way to Katahdin. It was great to have him back, and Orient greeted him like a long-lost friend. We talked for hours, getting caught up on everything that had happened since we had been together in the Whites, five weeks earlier.

The next morning, we enjoyed a colossal twelve-pancake breakfast at nearby Harrison's Camps, and then started on the Trail toward the little town of Caratunk. Indian summer was teasing us that day with seventy degrees and a gentle breeze.

At ten o'clock we took a break, and I thought about the people in my Sunday-school class back in Burlington. I knew that, right then, as they had every Sunday morning for the past eight months, they would be praying for Orient and me.

The Sunday before, they had remembered us as we started up Bigelow Mountain, and I knew their prayers had continued during the days we were stranded in the fire warden's cabin.

There is a lot I don't understand about prayer, but I am convinced that the Lord listens to His people and responds to their requests. My Uncle Gruder used to say, "The Lord takes care of fools and cripples." Maybe blind men were included as well.

Between Pierce Pond and Caratunk lay the mighty Kennebec River, the foremost water barrier without a bridge anywhere on the Appalachian Trail. I had been told it was dangerous to ford at best, and impassable many days of the year. The daily release from a hydroelectric plant upriver raised the level very quickly from waist-deep at low water to a depth of more than six feet. Few hikers still forded the river, and after a young woman drowned while attempting it in 1985, the MATC established a free ferry service for hikers. Even though the service for the 1990 season had ended on October 8, a contact in Caratunk had asked Steve Longley to take us across. We weren't sure he had gotten the message about our scheduled arrival that Sunday morning, November 4. If he wasn't there, we faced a twelve-mile walk downriver to the bridge at Bingham, and the same distance back on the other side.

As we reached the bottom of a steep hill on the south bank of the river, I heard a canoe scrape the rocks right in front of us. It was Steve. He told me the river was higher that day than it usually was during spring run-off, so he would have to take us one at a time. We agreed that I should go first, then Steve would return for Orient and make a third trip for Dave. Steve placed me in the front of the canoe with my pack in the middle and himself in back.

Orient whined a little back on shore as Steve and I paddled about thirty yards upriver in the calm water near the south bank. Steve described the Kennebec as one hundred yards wide and twelve to sixteen feet deep. We turned across the current and both paddled hard to keep from being carried too far downstream. Steve assured me that we were technically still on the A.T., because a white blaze was painted on the bottom of his canoe!

Once we were all across, we were met by Dan Hanson, a man who offered to slack-pack[1] us for the next five miles and then take us to his camp. (In Maine, a camp is what people in North Carolina call a cabin.) That night, he prepared a partridge for dinner, and we enjoyed a great evening together.

The temperature plummeted into the twenties before dawn, but we got an early start up Pleasant Pond Mountain. We made it all of the way to Joe's Hole Lean-to, where we had to work quickly to make camp because it was so cold. We bedded down early again that night.

The next day we traversed Moxie Bald Mountain in a thick, wet snow, wondering what the weather would do to the streams in front of us. The next afternoon, when we reached the West Branch of the Piscataquis River, we found out.

On another day, the water might have been trickling past, ankle deep. That afternoon, forty yards below the A.T. crossing, it thundered through giant rocks in a torrent of white foam. We had to shout at each other to be heard over it. Should we chance a crossing or not?

Half a mile back up the mountain, there was an old logging road we could follow five miles to Blanchard Village. There we could cross the Piscataquis on a bridge and follow a road a mile and half back to the A.T. That was a lot of extra walking and we were already beat. I asked Dave what he thought. He said the river looked fordable, if we took our time.

It was getting late and cold so we didn't have a lot of time to discuss the options. We decided to go for it.

It was a choice that almost cost us our lives.

I shuddered with my first step into the icy water, wishing I could run through to the other side, but moving

---

[1] To have someone else carry your pack.

slowly, my right arm linked with Dave's left, pack unbuckled in case the worst happened. I tried to talk myself across: "Plant the hiking stick, feel for a rock on the bottom, inch ahead, slowly, carefully, don't make a mistake."

I thought we were going to make it when Dave yelled and released his hold on my arm. The waist-deep current had swept him off his feet, and now he was in the water, fighting for the other side. Seconds later, the current took me, and I went under too. Fortunately, Orient, a strong swimmer, had no trouble crossing the turbulent stream.

I still don't know how both Dave and I made it across without losing our packs. That was a miracle. But once on the other side, we were far from safe. The sun was gone, the temperature was below freezing, and we were both soaked from head to foot. With water sloshing in our boots, we started up the ridge, trying to generate body heat while looking for a place to make camp.

That night, shivering in our tent, I struggled with whether we should press on. There could be a dozen more difficult water crossings between us and Katahdin. How could we keep fording waist-deep rivers in freezing weather?

Besides, contact with people on the hike — part of what I thought my hiking "mission" was — seemed to be over. We hadn't met one person on the Trail in the past three days. With one stop in Monson and then the Hundred Mile Wilderness to Katahdin, the likelihood of meeting hikers in November was almost nil. Did I want to keep going for my own selfish motives and the honor of having completed the Trail? Was it worth the risk to try and make it the rest of the way?

I asked the Lord to show me what to do. "If it's Your will for us to stop the hike at this point, please let me know. If You want us to keep going north, please let me know that. I leave it in Your hands."

Within two minutes, I realized that I was completely warm all over. Usually, it took two hours just to get my feet warm. I felt that warming my body so quickly was God's way of giving me the sign to continue. I told Dave I thought we should keep going, and he said he was with me all the way. I had no idea how we were going to do it, but I knew the Lord would show us the answer in His time.

The next day, Friday, November 9, we hit Monson and the warm hospitality of Shaw's Boarding House. Since opening their door to hikers in 1978, Keith and Pat Shaw had become legends along the Trail. I had been looking forward to meeting them since I left Georgia. They fed us enormous amounts of food, and Keith seasoned the meals with stories that made me laugh harder than I had in weeks.

The best story was Keith's account of a thru-hiker who had taken full advantage of their all-you-can-eat breakfast. In an effort to prove his mettle, the young man had consumed a total of twenty eggs, along with bacon, a whole package of donuts, toast, coffee, orange juice, and a quart of milk.

"He turned white as a sheet," Keith said "and folded up like an accordion on the floor right next to the table. He lay there for two and a half hours before crawling upstairs on his hands and knees." The hiker stayed two more days, trying to recover, and left without eating another thing.

Keith's story confirmed the opinion of many people that "crazy thru-hiker" was a redundant term!

The first night at Shaw's, we met a young man named Al from Illinois. He had left Abol Bridge ten days before, planning to hike all the way south to Springer Mountain. He was young and strong and had all the latest gear, but the Hundred Mile Wilderness had convinced him this was no time to be hiking in Maine. He talked about the rough terrain and said there were hundreds of blowdowns across the Trail. In some places, he had experienced great difficulty finding the way. He was headed home the next day.

I knew that if Dave and I were going to make it to Katahdin, we needed some advice and help. The Hundred Mile Wilderness was just that — the most remote and inaccessible portion of the entire A.T. From Monson to Abol Bridge, the A.T. did not cross a paved road or come near a telephone or town. Most guidebooks recommended carrying a minimum of ten days' food, because resupply was not an option.

That Friday night, I called Art Batchelder in New Hampshire and took him up on his offer to give us a hand through the last hundred miles. AB had just completed that part of the Trail and knew the conditions as well as anyone. After he arrived the next day, we came up with a timetable and a plan.

Art had a four-wheel drive vehicle and detailed maps of the logging roads throughout the Hundred Mile Wilderness. He said it was remote but remained accessible as long as we didn't have a big snow. We arranged to meet over the next ten days at six places where he could resupply us with food and check on our progress. If the weather became life-threatening, he could drive us out to a nearby town and take us back to the Trail after the storm cleared.

On Saturday night, park director, Buzz Caverly, and his assistant, Jean Hookwater, drove down from Millinocket and offered to help any way they could. I just couldn't get over the time and effort Buzz was devoting to helping me finish the hike. Every time I thanked him for something he'd done, he downplayed his efforts, saying, "Small job, Bill. Small job."

During dinner, Buzz and Keith Shaw swapped stories about deer poachers in the north woods. Buzz described breakneck chases in a '49 Ford V-8 across darkened fields, trying to catch deer poachers in the act. Keith countered Buzz's stories by describing his adventures of eluding game wardens by hiding in the low branches of thick evergreens. Before the evening was over, I think they decided that they had probably been on opposite sides of at least one chase.

Buzz was refreshing to be around. He always had a smile in his voice. Baxter State Park was his life and he loved to tell stories about the early days. As a young ranger, he once set up a water pump not far from his cabin with a sign that read, "Old Tracey's Spring." The pump was real, but it wasn't connected to anything. When hikers came in complaining that the pump didn't work, he told them they'd have to prime it with water from the nearby pond. Of course, the priming produced no results. If they bothered to open the wooden box next to the pump, they found an old bed spring and a sign that said, "Keep Smiling."

Buzz had a lot of fun with this, until the day his superior tried the pump and finally opened the box in frustration. He put Buzz on probation. "Of course," Buzz said with a laugh, "I was on probation for the first ten years!"

As I listened to Buzz's stories, I realized how much he had given up to become the director of Baxter State Park in 1982. He loved trails and ponds, not telephones and paperwork. But more than anything, he loved the two hundred thousand-acre park that Governor Percival Baxter had left as a legacy to the people of Maine. Buzz was committed to preserving it as a wilderness so future generations could enjoy it. The task kept him behind a desk far more than he wanted, but he did it as a labor of love.

Just as we finished dessert at Shaw's, several hunters arrived to spend the night. Buzz was sitting with his back to the door as they walked in, and Keith said, "Are you boys ready to go out and jack (poach) a few deer?"

They responded with a hearty "You bet!" just as Buzz turned around with his badge in full view. "How're you doing?" he said with a big smile. I laughed so hard that I almost fell out of my chair.

Many thru-hikers said that the hardest thing in Maine was leaving Shaw's. We stayed an extra day, trying to get organized for the final push. The timetable we had worked out called for hiking eight to ten miles a day through the Hundred Mile Wilderness. It seemed workable, and I was committed to pushing myself to the limit to make it happen.

On Sunday morning, Orient, Dave, and I hit the Trail, armed with a lot of optimism and a secret weapon we had purchased at the general store in Monson. It seemed so obvious, we couldn't figure out why none of the guidebooks ever mentioned it. Now we had a way to ford rivers without getting wet.

We walked through freezing rain all morning, passed Leeman Brook Lean-to just after noon, and pressed on toward the logging road where Art was supposed to meet us. About three in the afternoon, the rain changed to big lumps of wet snow, and by four o'clock, we were standing at the top of Little Wilson Falls. The light was beginning to fade and we still had a mile to go before meeting Art.

The steep, rocky path down to the bottom of the Falls was covered with ice, and I fell several times before deciding I had to slow down. With a sinking feeling, we discussed the fact that we had not agreed on how long Art should wait for us at the logging road. We had even suggested that, in case of bad weather, we might not hike past Leeman Brook Lean-to. He had no way of knowing where we were or how long he should wait.

When we reached the ford across Little Wilson Stream, it was almost dark, and time to use the secret weapon. Dave and I tied thirty-gallon trash bags as high as we could on our legs and stepped into the icy water. We were already planning an article about our new stream-crossing technique for the *Appalachian Trailway News*. For reasons still unknown to me, the bags leaked immediately, and offered no protection at all. Mine filled with water, so besides trying to cross the knee-deep stream, I was pulling at least twenty gallons of water with each leg. We managed to cross without falling, and, in our haste to meet Art, failed to fill our water bottles.

It was dark and snowing heavily as we started up the last half-mile toward the logging road. Hopefully, Art would still be there with the engine running and the heater on, and we could go somewhere warm and dry for the night. When we reached the logging road, Dave saw fresh tire tracks, but no Art.

It was our fault for not being more definite about how long he should wait. We set up the tent as the snow continued to fall, covered our packs with the trash bags, and tried to make the best of a very discouraging situation. Dave headed back down to the stream for water, but returned empty-handed twenty minutes later, saying he had become completely disoriented in the snow and knew he wasn't thinking clearly.

With all four water bottles empty and no apparent water source nearby, we settled for some dried fruit for supper. Art had Orient's food, so I gave Orient some "cookies," and he shivered along with us in the tent.

Some time during the night, the snow changed to driving rain, and soon we realized that our tent was sitting in two inches of water. The condensation inside from two men and an eighty-pound dog was almost as great as the rain seeping in from the outside. It ranked near the top of our list of most miserable nights on the Trail.

The next morning, when we tried to heat some collected rainwater, my stove leaked fuel and ignited in a ball of fire. Orient quickly left the tent and headed somewhere out of danger. We had to eat granola bars for breakfast. I offered Orient some "cookies" but he ignored them and wasn't acting normal at all. As we broke camp and packed to leave, he curled up about thirty yards away from us, refusing to drink water or have anything to do with us. (In the light, we had discovered we were only twenty yards from a pond.)

We started up the Trail after leaving a note on the A.T. sign in case Art returned. The hills around us were gushing water as if a giant had walked through, puncturing them with a sharpened pole. Up on the ridge, the Trail was flowing like a stream from the run-off alone. Ahead of us that day were Thompson Brook, Big Wilson Stream, Wilbur Brook, Vaughn Stream, and Long Pond Stream. Two weeks earlier, a hiker had been swept off her feet while trying to cross Vaughn Stream, and she was almost carried over the falls. In my usual fashion, I committed the day to the Lord and asked Him to work things out the way He wanted them.

As we climbed the ridge, I thought I heard someone shout. Dave said he hadn't heard anything. Fifteen minutes later, we both heard the voice — and it was Art. He had a thermos of hot coffee, candy bars, and an explanation of what had happened the night before.

Because of high water, he had left his vehicle and hiked two miles in to the Trail crossing. He waited for us until an hour after dark, then left, assuming we had stayed at the lean-to. That morning, he had tried to find an alternate route into the logging road, and ended up hiking back in the same way.

When I asked him about the tire tracks, he said there were six hunters staying in a cabin half a mile down the logging road from where we had tented. I sure wished we'd known that the night before.

Art told us there was no way we could cross the streams ahead of us that day, but we could follow the route of the old A.T. along the road, and cross on bridges. We headed for his vehicle and, as we passed the hunters' cabin, they invited us in for breakfast. I downed my bacon, eggs and hot coffee sitting in a chair with my feet inside the oven, warm and dry. Total luxury.

The next morning we were back on the Trail with a better arrangement for a road-crossing rendezvous with Art two days later. A fierce wind raked the top of Barren Mountain, making the old fire tower pull against its cables like a chained animal. A five-minute break in the trees just below the summit left us shivering with cold.

We reached Cloud Pond Lean-to just after noon, and debated the merits of staying there or pressing on to Chairback Gap Lean-to, seven miles away. If we could average one and a half miles an hour, we could reach Chairback Gap by 5:00 p.m., just about the time it would get completely dark. We kept going, saying it was the only way we would ever finish the hike.

The storm the night before had left eight inches of snow in the Barren-Chairback Range. In some ways, it made the Trail easier because the rocks and roots were not exposed. But across the treeless summits, the Trail was marked with blazes painted on the rocky surface that was now buried beneath the snow. Without cairns or blazes to follow, Orient was having a very difficult time finding the Trail. At least with Dave along, we had another pair of eyes.

At 5:30, we switched on our headlamps and saw a sign saying Chairback Gap Lean-to, 3.8 miles. Had it taken us the past five hours to come three miles? Surely the signs were wrong!

The temperature dropped into the twenties and the wind continued to howl as we trudged toward Third Mountain and Columbus Mountain. Several times we backtracked on the treeless, snow-covered summits and wandered the perimeter before relocating the Trail. Other than a couple of candy bars and some beef jerky, we hadn't eaten anything all day.

When Dave said something about the foolishness of putting ourselves in this kind of life-threatening situation,

I cut him off. "I'm prepared to do this every day between now and Katahdin if I have to."

But I knew that, if one of us took a bad fall or turned an ankle, we were in serious trouble.

A few minutes later, I stepped through the thin ice of a partially frozen bog and sank in halfway to my knees. The snow-covered crust had supported Orient's weight but had given way under mine. I felt the cold water fill my boots, and my feet quickly lost all feeling. I wanted to stop, but knew it would be insane to try and set up the tent in that wind. We had to reach the shelter, but I didn't know how much longer I could keep going.

At 7:30 p.m., we still had two miles to go, and sleet was beginning to sting my face. I stopped to catch my breath and felt the Trail moving under my feet. Thinking I was dizzy, I put my hand on a tree. The trunk was swaying so much in the wind that the roots under the Trail were heaving up and down, trying to break free from the soil. We had to keep moving.

The memory of the previous night without water caused us to stop beside a trickle falling from a rock next to the Trail. The caps on our water bottles were frozen solid and we had to knock them against a tree to loosen them. Inside each bottle, the ice was half an inch thick.

At 9:30 p.m., we finally stumbled into Chairback Gap Lean-to. After hiking non-stop for fourteen hours, we had covered eleven and one half miles. Once inside the lean-to, I fumbled with my pack, unable to open a zippered pocket or to remove my sleeping bag from its straps underneath.

A sixty mile-an-hour wind howled into the open side of the lean-to, so Dave used his pack as a windbreak for the stove and made some hot cocoa. I drank two cups but still couldn't get warm.

My fingers were numb and completely useless. I couldn't untie my boot laces or unzip my sleeping bag. Being blind, I was already without one of my five senses.

Losing the sense of touch and use of my hands rendered me completely helpless. Dave helped me remove my boots and get into my sleeping bag.

If I had been alone that night, I would have died.

Even in my sleeping bag, I continued to shake for an hour. Dave fixed a "yuppie" dinner, ate half, and handed the rest to me. My thinking was so confused I didn't even want to eat. He told me I had to: The hot food was exactly what my body needed to generate some warmth. An hour before midnight, I fell into an exhausted sleep.

Throughout the night, the fierce wind and bitter cold created a wind chill of -36 degrees F. The next morning, our sleeping bags were covered with half an inch of snow. Orient had curled up in the back corner of the shelter, but even he couldn't escape a covering of white.

After breakfast, I spent an hour thawing my boots over the stove before putting them on. It was 10:30 a.m. by the time we got packed up and out of the shelter. We hoped Art was waiting for us at the road crossing five miles away. If he wasn't, the next shelter was five additional miles on the other side of the West Branch of the Pleasant River. Even if the river was only waist-deep, it would be suicide to ford it in the numbing cold.

Halfway to the road crossing, I said aloud, "We aren't going to cross any more rivers in this weather. I believe the Lord wants us to finish the Trail, but He also wants us to be smart about it." Dave agreed and so did Art when we met him at St. Regis Road.

Before I told Art of my conclusion, he said, "I'm glad you guys made it the last two days in this weather, but I have something to tell you. If you insist on continuing this hike the way you're doing it now, you're going to have to find someone else to help you, because I'm not interested in helping you get killed."

Chapter Eighteen

Doing It His Way

The lady at K.C.'s Place was the most honest waitress I'd met in a long time. When I asked if their french fries were greasy, she said, "Of course. They're deep-fat fried. How could they be anything *but* greasy?"

Most people in cafes were apologetic about their fried foods and denied any remote association with grease. For a hiker, fat meant calories and energy. I asked for a big order of fries with my cheeseburger, and some onion rings, too.

They were the best french fries I'd had in weeks.

Sitting at the counter, I could hear several people, so I asked them if there were any motels nearby. They said no, but suggested we call a bed and breakfast in Brownville Junction, a couple of miles away. Art tried, but there was no answer.

We didn't need anything fancy, just a place to spend the night and try to figure out how to approach the remaining miles to Katahdin. It was the twelfth of November and I still couldn't give people a reliable estimate of when this hike was going to end. My family and friends from church had to make travel plans, and I wanted answers for the press. Most of all, I needed some clear idea of how in the world we could keep going north in the bitter cold without fording any streams.

Since there weren't any motels, maybe a church in Brownville Junction would let us sleep in their basement. It wouldn't hurt to ask. It was almost sundown when we knocked at the parsonage of the United Methodist Church. Rev. Ron Chaffee told me it was fine with him, but he needed to clear it with the members of the church board. He invited us in for hot coffee and cake while he went to the phone.

The cake was great and Ron told us it came from a Celebration of Life that he had held yesterday for a member of the church. "I never have liked the term 'funeral,'" he said, "so I call it a Celebration of Life. When a Christian dies and goes to be with the Lord, he's more alive than he's ever been."

I liked this preacher already.

Half an hour later, everything was all set and he took us to the basement of the little church next door, our home for the night. As we passed through the kitchen, Art pointed to a newspaper article pinned to a bulletin board: "Orient Express Makes Its Way to Katahdin." Ron said one of the children's Sunday school classes had been following the hike of a blind man and his dog on the Appalachian Trail. He stopped in the middle of his sentence, and I believe that was the first time he realized that *I* was the man.

That evening, Art spread his maps out on the kitchen table and outlined the problems as he saw them. The weather forecast called for continued cold, with lows in the twenties and thirties. Parts of the Gulf Hagas Trail would likely be under water because of the recent storms. The East Branch of the Pleasant River was a major ford with no road access on either side. If we hit it on the Trail, the only way was through it. This would be nearly impossible in current conditions. Other streams and pond outlets that were normally just trickles could easily be hip-deep now.

Art proposed a plan that would enable us to cover nearly fifty miles on old logging roads, then rejoin the A.T.

with thirty miles left to Katahdin. If we could cover the logging roads in a little more than two days and make ten miles a day on the Trail, we could be at Daicey Pond by November 19th. It sounded like the only reasonable solution to me, and we all agreed to start the next day.

While Art was at the parsonage making some phone calls, Ron came over with one of the children's Sunday-school teachers. She wanted to take a picture of Orient and me to show to the kids in her class the next Sunday. They had been following our progress since August and she said they prayed for us every week. Ron told me a little about the young people in the church and wondered if there was any way we could return the next Sunday and take part in the service. I told him that if we could work it out, we'd be there.

Before eating our supper, we read Hebrews 13:1-2,

"Keep on loving each other as brothers. Do not forget to entertain strangers, for by so doing, some people have entertained angels without knowing it." (NIV)

I didn't feel very celestial, but I knew that Ron and Sue and the people in their congregation were bound to encounter some angels before long, because their doors and their hearts were open.

That night, I spread my sleeping bag on a long table that the younger children used for Sunday school. Orient curled up on a little mat under the table and gave a big sigh right before he fell asleep. I listened to the wind rattling the windows and thanked the Lord for the people in this church who were willing to let three strangers and a dog sleep in their basement.

The next morning, Art dropped us off with a set of directions for where to turn on the next twenty miles of snow-covered road. In some places, he said, there would be a sign marking a snowmobile route. In others, we would have to estimate distance and turn on what we judged to be the right crossroad. It wasn't foolproof by any means. He promised to meet us by sundown and headed off to take care of some details in town.

About noon, we reached a stretch of road that was covered with ice, and stopped to put on our crampons[1]. The small steel spikes fit under our boot heels and enabled us to keep going at a steady pace. Without them, we would have been sliding all over the road and would have had great difficulty going up and down the hills.

It was a miracle we had them at all.

On the evening of November 1, I was staying at the Stratton Inn after being "rescued" from the fire warden's cabin on Bigelow Mountain. Dave had found out where I was and called from Newark, New Jersey, to finalize our plans to meet on the Trail. As I was talking to him, Peter Martel told me, "Have Dave go to Campmor and get some crampons before he leaves."

The next morning, Dave drove through the New York City rush-hour traffic to Campmor's main store in Paramus, New Jersey. I had told him to get instep crampons, but for some reason he bought heel crampons instead — the last two pair they had. Then he dashed down the turnpike to make his plane to Bangor.

The crampons were in our packs when we hit the ice that afternoon, and they were exactly what we needed. Instep crampons would have been extremely dangerous for Orient: I followed him so closely that several times a day I would step on his right hind paw with my left foot. On the Trail, he would give a little yelp and I'd apologize. If I had been wearing instep crampons, my apology wouldn't have done any good.

I remembered Peter Putnam's story of the man who stepped on his Seeing Eye dog's paw with the deadly steel spikes. Even after being rushed to a veterinarian, the dog had bled to death. Heel crampons lessened the danger for Orient, but I slowed down and gave him more space, just to be sure.

---

[1]A pair of spiked iron plates fastened on shoes to prevent slipping.

Late that afternoon, we crossed the East Branch of the Pleasant river. I stopped for a minute on the old wooden bridge and listened to the water churning over the rocks below. It sounded as if we were in the right place — above it, not in it.

By 4:30, we had covered twenty-two miles, but there was no sign of Art. We should have learned from the last time that things could go wrong, but we had left ourselves completely unprepared if he was unable to return. We had left our packs behind, and carried only water and a light lunch. Neither of us had a match to start a fire. As long as we kept moving, we could keep warm, but after twenty-two miles, we were ready to drop.

Just before dark, Orient heard something behind us, and soon the lights of Art's jeep came over the hill. We had been saved from our own folly once again. Art apologized for being a little late, and handed us a thermos of hot coffee. He had driven nearly two hundred miles that day and spent a great deal of time on the phone, trying to make sure the next few days would go according to plan. That Aht was a real Maine-ah.

No matter where Orient sat in the jeep, he managed to stretch his head across Art's lap. The two of them were great friends. Orient promptly went to sleep as Art drove us to a beautiful A-frame on Lower Jo-Mary Lake, where Buzz Caverly had arranged for us to spend the night.

Inside the camp, Orient wolfed down his dinner, then collapsed on the carpet, out for the night. I couldn't get used to the luxury of taking off my boots and putting my feet up next to a warm stove.

If I was really freezing to death somewhere in a lean-to, I didn't want to wake up from this dream.

The following day we hiked another twenty miles, half of it with crampons. That night, Buzz and his wife, Jan, came by the camp with "pizzers and soders." We were a long drive from Millinocket, where they lived, but Buzz still insisted it was a small job. He had a clipboard full of messages from reporters, Carolyn, Trail friends, and my kids. I could tell he had spent most of the day on the phone making arrangements for the end of the hike, if it ever came.

After Buzz and Jan left, I found a cassette tape in my food box. It was labeled, "Letters to Bill Irwin," and came from a class of third and fourth grade students in Burlington. A friend had read their letters onto a tape.

The letters were classics and just as sweet as they could be. I got the biggest kick from a little girl who wrote: "I'm glad that you're almost done with that Trail. It would not be fun to walk 20,000 miles."

She was the first person who knew how long the Trail felt to me.

The teacher said her favorite question came from a little boy who asked: "Since he's blind, how will he know when he gets to the end of the Trail?" She couldn't answer it, and I wasn't sure I could either.

I did know that the next day we'd be back on the A.T. with less than thirty miles to go. I could be finished by Thanksgiving if, as Keith Shaw said, "The Lord's willing and the devil don't mind."

Once again, it wasn't as simple as I had planned. The next morning, we made a wrong turn in Art's jeep and drove around for an hour and a half before finally locating Pollywog Stream. It seemed I was doomed to late starts on the Trail in spite of all our best efforts to get off early. Every hour we lost in the morning increased the possibility of hiking after dark, and I wasn't interested in any more of that.

Two days on the even surface of logging roads had spoiled me. For the first two miles along Rainbow Stream, I complained about the rocks, roots and 'rosion. After getting that out of my system, the only thing I had to worry about was how we were going to get across the stream.

We stopped for lunch at Rainbow Stream Lean-to and Dave read the shelter register to me. The last entries by northbound hikers were three weeks old. AB Positive, Mr. Moleskin, Midnight Express, Cruise Control, and Daddy Longlegs had each jotted a brief note as they pressed on toward Katahdin. Al, the young man we met at Shaw's, had been the last person to sign the register. He had spent the night alone there on October 31, full of enthusiasm for his southbound thru-hike.

Winter has a way of quickly changing things in Maine!

On the day we had left Monson, a party of three hikers had headed south from Katahdin, determined to hike twenty miles a day and carry only five days' rations. Every guidebook urged hikers not to enter the Hundred Mile Wilderness with less than ten days' food. Too many things could go wrong. The trio covered forty miles in five days before hiking out on a logging road and calling Keith Shaw to come get them.

Just outside the shelter, I put my hand against a huge birch tree and laughed out loud. Someone had put an electrical outlet with a plastic cover into the trunk. It reminded me of the telephone with its cord inserted into a log at the Jerry Cabin shelter in Tennessee. Hikers knew the phone couldn't possibly work, but they couldn't resist lifting the receiver just to check.

Ten yards below the shelter, two ice-covered logs spanned the rushing Rainbow Stream. This was the kind of place where a hiker in a hurry could find himself suddenly wet and in trouble. Orient scampered across alone, and I inched to the other side on my hands and knees. Months before, I had told Warren Doyle I'd crawl to Maine if I had to. If he could only see me now!

One lyrical hiker wrote: "In Maine, Lady Winter is beautiful and alluring, but not to be trusted. One day she whispers a gentle invitation and flashes you a quick, sunny smile. 'Come along,' she says. 'We'll have fun.' The next day, she turns on you, becoming icy, angry and aloof. Flirt with her if you like. Court her if you will. Love her if you must. But don't trust her. Don't ever trust her."

Rainbow Lake was rimmed with ice as we skirted it throughout the afternoon. Once again, Buzz had found a roof in the wilderness for us, and we walked in to the Rainbow Camps an hour before dark. The camps were not open to hikers, but the owners graciously offered us one of their cabins for the night. Herb and Lynne Stufflebeam, the caretakers, welcomed us. Two company executives invited Dave and me to join them and a weekend guest for supper. Soon we were feasting on moose steaks, broiled chicken, hot biscuits and stuffed squash. For dessert, Lynne produced a freshly baked apple pie. What kind of hardship was this? I felt guilty all the way through my second huge piece.

We quickly established a bond of friendship as they asked questions about why I was making the hike and how Orient and I had negotiated difficult parts of the Trail. When I told them that I couldn't take one step without the Lord's help, one of the men answered, with a catch in his voice, "I know exactly what you mean."

He told me his beautiful nineteen-year-old daughter was slowly recovering from severe brain damage suffered in an automobile accident several months before. He said their family had been sustained by the grace of God and the help and prayers of hundreds of people. I was deeply touched by her courage and by his willingness to share a very personal story with me, a total stranger.

On November 17, we covered the final stretch of the Hundred Mile Wilderness and crossed the Penobscot River at Abol Bridge. Art was waiting to drive us back to Brownville Junction for church services the next day. Rev. Ron Chaffee had asked me to give the children's story in church and I had decided to tell them about finding the way on the trail of life.

Tom and Nancy Belvin welcomed us into their home in Brownville Junction on Saturday night, and fixed a real Southern meal. Before marrying Nancy, Tom had lived in Birmingham, Alabama, so we had a lot of things to reminisce about. When we sat down for supper, Nancy handed me a bowl of fried okra. I thought I'd died and gone to Alabama.

When Orient and I stood up in church the next morning, the kids all giggled. It was probably the first time they'd had a dog in church, at least with permission. I held up a white blaze on a piece of construction paper and told them how the hikers on the Appalachian Trail followed the marks on the trees and rocks. They were the only directions a person needed to get all the way from Georgia to Maine.

"What did you have to do to stay on the Trail?" I asked. They all knew the answer: See the blazes and follow them. But, I said, if a person ignored those white marks, they wouldn't do him a bit of good. Then I asked, "Wouldn't it be wonderful if it was that easy to find our way in life? You'd just follow the blazes from one goal to the next."

They agreed, and I told them that God had marked the trail for us — His blazes were in the Bible.

To the kids it was perfectly clear. If we read the Bible but ignore its message, it doesn't do us any good. But if we follow God's word and live it, He leads us along His trail to eternal life.

I visited with the children during their Sunday-school class downstairs, and they enjoyed meeting Orient and giving him lots of hugs. Orient loved it, too. When they sang for us, I was amazed to hear Christmas songs. I had started hiking a month before Easter and now these children were singing about shepherds watching their flocks by night.

I thought back to one afternoon when I had asked the Lord if it was time to quit because I wouldn't be meeting any more people along the Trail. He had said, "Keep going," because He knew who was just ahead. I couldn't have planned it, but, just like the rest of the hike, He had made it happen His way.

Chapter Nineteen

The Real Story

Monday, November 19, I was awake at 5:30 a.m., wondering why I couldn't sleep. Several friends had joined Art, Dave, and me at Daicey Pond, and we planned to hike seven and one-half miles that day, southbound from Daicey to Abol Bridge. Mentally, I knew that I had only ten miles left to complete my hike. Emotionally, I was torn between the desire to finish and the realization that an unrepeatable chapter in my life was about to end.

A lot of things were going through my head by now. I thought a lot about the Indians who had gone before me. I thought about Pamola. I thought about Thoreau, and how he'd tried four times to climb Katahdin. I couldn't believe I could do it and Thoreau couldn't!

My thoughts were, also, that it was over. There was just a cursory piece left, and a lot of people were going to share it with me. I realized again how amazing it was that I had met all of these people during the last week, when I had thought the "people experience" part of my trek was supposed to be over.

I thought about finishing the Trail in one piece. It had always been in the back of my mind that I might have to stop for some reason, although I never considered that my death could be one of those reasons.

And my mind kept going back to people and places along the Trail.

During my time in Damascus, Virginia, I had talked with a young blind woman who had applied for a Seeing Eye dog. Talking with Orient and me and hearing about our hike had answered a lot of her questions about how independent she could become with a dog guide. I had been where she was, and knew the doubts and fears that preyed on her mind. She touched me with her courage and willingness to risk enlarging the horizons of her life.

Another great encouragement was Bob Barker, who suffers from multiple sclerosis, yet has thru-hiked the A.T. three times on crutches. I had watched the documentary film, *Five Million Steps*, which showed him climbing mountains and carrying his pack, while describing how his faith enabled him to keep going. Every time I struggled down a steep descent or crossed a boulder field, I had wondered how in the world Bob Barker made it across. This had kept me from complaining more than I did, and had fired my will to keep going.

I decided that thru-hikers needed encouragement all along the way because it was impossible to prepare mentally and physically for six months of life on the Trail. Trying to tell a prospective thru-hiker about the pain of his coming journey seemed like telling a woman in her first pregnancy that during childbirth she would experience some discomfort.

Lying there at Daicey Pond, I couldn't begin to estimate how many people along the way had shown their kindness and interest. Hundreds? A couple of thousand? Sometimes it was a handshake, a hug, a word of recognition or some expression of thanks to Orient and me. A cold drink, an apple, or a ride into town was often the greatest thing anyone could have given us at the time. Being welcomed at church services along the way and included in family meals had put us back on the Trail thankful and encouraged.

The two-way radio crackled to life about 8:00 a.m. with the familiar voice of Buzz Caverly. He was on the way in and I knew it was time for me to get a move on. My family and some friends from church were beginning to arrive at the Big Moose Inn outside Millinocket for a victory celebration that would be held on Wednesday. Members of the press had booked several rooms and were bringing in a satellite dish for some live television interviews. Buzz and his staff were working eighteen hours a day to coordinate all the comings and goings in Baxter Park. Things were getting a little crazy.

When Carolyn Starling arrived, we hugged for five minutes before she stopped crying. For nearly nine months, she had been the first one to deal with every good and bad event in my life. Even though we talked weekly, it had been six months since we'd seen each other. I wasn't sure she was crying because she was glad to see me or relieved because she could start spending her evenings somewhere besides on the phone.

Without all her work and support, Orient and I never would have made it.

Throughout my hike, reporters had focused their attention on Orient and me, but I wish I could have convinced them that the real story was the hundreds of people whose names and faces would never make the news. They were the ones who had inspired me to keep going and who had kept me on the Trail with their work and their prayers. I had had a wonderful support team back in North Carolina and another spread out all along the way. In every state, God had deepened my trust in Him while renewing my faith in people as well.

And then there was Orient. What an example of unselfish love! He lived to lead and found his freedom in the harness that called him to give the best he had to someone else. That was another piece in the puzzle of what my hike was all about.

A local veterinarian came out to give Orient a thorough examination and pronounced him in excellent condition. Rumors of his poor health and even mistreatment had continued to persist throughout the hike, in spite of regular examinations and care. This would put the gossip to rest and hopefully head off any feelings that might tarnish Orient's reward for completing the Trail.

I thought back to the night two years earlier, when Orient and I had left The Seeing Eye for the first time as a team. On the way home, we stopped in the Washington, D.C. area to visit friends to whom I had given my previous dog guide, Sailor. Sailor had been retired because of a back problem. He could still walk and made a great pet, but he was unable to perform the rigorous, daily physical duties required of a dog guide. It was a little unorthodox to bring Orient into the same house with Sailor, but it was a visit I needed to make.

I hadn't seen Sailor in three months, but, of course, he recognized me right away. After our initial greeting, he kept looking at me and then at Orient's harness, and I could almost picture what was going through his mind. Was I back to get him? Were we going home? Who was this other dog?

After supper, while everyone was interested in a football game on TV, I removed the harness from Orient and asked one of my friends to hold his leash. I called Sailor quietly and we left the house together. Once outside, I slipped Orient's harness over Sailor's head and was amazed to feel him come to life. We started walking down the road in the cold air and I could tell he was glad to be working again.

When he took me around a low hanging branch, I praised him. "Sailor, what a good boy you are!" He stuck his head straight up in the air and acted as if he was the most important dog in the world.

We must have walked for two miles, out and back, before we re-entered the house and I took the harness off him for the last time. In a harness that many dogs would consider a prison, Sailor had recaptured his reason for living. In a role that some would call subservient, he had felt truly free.

Buzz and his staff made several trips over the icy roads into the park, making sure everyone arrived safely. About 10:00 a.m., we struck out on the Trail to Abol Bridge. The trek started in typical fashion with the people in the lead talking, laughing, and heading down the wrong trail. When Orient started walking hesitantly, I asked if anyone could see a white blaze. Sure enough, we were on a blue-blazed side trail. We backtracked a quarter of a mile and managed to stay on the A.T. for the rest of the day.

An angry overcast spit snow on us most of the day. Lunch on the Trail followed the usual sweat-stop-freeze pattern, and I was anxious to keep moving. When we reached Katahdin Stream, it was a mass of surging white water. Fortunately, someone had rigged an L-shaped log bridge across it. Unfortunately, the logs were covered with ice. It took nearly an hour to get everyone across, and Orient absolutely refused to swim the stream until everyone else had walked on and I was able to coax him across. I decided it was impossible to have a dull day anywhere on the A.T.

Al Dale and an ABC news crew joined us for the last couple of miles to cover the end of that day's hike. During a wrap-up interview in the little store at Abol Bridge, Al asked me: "What message are people supposed to get from your hike?" In effect, he was asking me the question again: "What does all this mean?"

What a question! It reminded me of the questions in the cereal-box contests when I was a kid. The winning response had to be original, clear, and creative — in twenty-five words or less.

What did it all mean? What was the message?

I took a deep breath and said: "It means that Jesus Christ died on the Cross for our sins and that, if we'll believe in Him and surrender ourselves to Him, He'll lead us and help us through life."

I knew that probably wasn't the answer Al wanted and was pretty sure they couldn't use it on the ABC news, but it was the only way I could sum it all up.

When a person says yes to the Lord and agrees to follow Him, God will move heaven and earth to help that person stay on His path. What God did for me on the Appalachian Trail was just a picture of what He longs to do for everyone who will walk with Him one step at a time.

I shuddered to think how easily I could have missed it all.

Chapter Twenty

The End of the Road

The next day, we decided to play all day. Then, on Wednesday, November 21, we woke to a clear blue "Carolina sky." It was the day before Thanksgiving in northern Maine. The temperature was in the mid-thirties and Katahdin stood as a snow-crowned backdrop, towering above the icy surface of Daicey Pond.

Noodles sounded good for breakfast, because I just couldn't manage another bowl of oatmeal, even on the last day of the hike. I wasn't sure what I was going to eat for the rest of my life, but could think of a couple of things that would be way down on the menu. I hadn't even washed the breakfast dishes before the first wave of people began rolling in.

I went outside and talked with a crew from NBC, and also a CBS affiliate in Bangor. The questions came in waves: "Are you anxious to finish the hike? What does it feel like to be done? Are you going to miss the Trail? What was the hardest part? What's your next big hike? The Pacific Crest Trail? The Continental Divide? What does Orient think about all this?"

While I talked to reporters, Buzz and his staff made several trips over the icy roads into the park, making sure everyone arrived safely. About 10:00 a.m., we struck out on the final two and a half miles.

It was wonderful to hear the voices of my family who had come thousands of miles to share this day together. Fifteen people from my church had driven thirty-six hours from Burlington to finish the Trail with me and celebrate God's faithfulness together. There's no way to describe what their presence meant to me that day.

In the end, there must have been close to one hundred of us strung out along this small portion of the Trail. A crew of Boy Scouts came along to help people negotiate the rocks across the two small streams along the way. Behind me, the sounds rose and fell as people enjoyed talking together, then were silenced by the beauty around them.

A tenth of a mile before the finish line at Katahdin Stream Campground, Buzz asked Orient and me to stop while the rest of the crowd went ahead. I guess it was right that Orient and I should walk the last stretch as we began, just the two of us and the Lord. It was another one of those moments of near completion that was overshadowed by the joy of the process.

I felt as if we were counting down the final seconds of a game in which victory had long been assured. At the gun, there would be a few moments of shouting, but the real satisfaction would lie in looking back over the whole contest and in remembering everyone who had contributed to the victory.

I rubbed Orient's head and wondered what he was thinking. Could he have any idea that this was the end? Without laying a lot of human emotion on him, I was sure of one thing: Orient's sense of joy and accomplishment was all wrapped up in me. He led me out of love, not out of a sense of duty or because of physical rewards. His victory was in faithfulness, willingly accepting his harness every morning and guiding me safely across whatever the Trail held for that day.

I couldn't imagine being as close to another dog as I was to Orient. God had given him the capacity for love and loyalty, and he had eagerly shared that with me. The Trail had molded us into a team, and I was proud to be part of the Orient Express.

Orient stepped out quickly on the snow-packed road. He seemed sure of his own feet and mine, so we covered the ground in long strides. As we neared the crowd, the people from my church began singing, and Orient slowed his pace. Everyone joined in on the first verse of *Amazing Grace*, and then there was silence.

I tugged on Orient's harness to further slow his pace. The closer we got to the finish line, the more I wanted to savor the moment. Just like every other thru-hiker, I wanted the hike to be finished, but I didn't want it to end. But now, against all the odds, in spite of all the predictions, because of all the love and prayers, it was done.

Orient quickened his steps and raised his eyes toward Katahdin when he was stopped in his tracks by voices from the crowd:

"The sign is on your left! You made it! It's done!"

Orient turned and led me to the familiar wooden sign, the last one on the Appalachian Trail for me. The crowd fell silent as I reached out, touched the sign, and dropped to my knees.

Incredibly, it was over.

Orient lay beside me as I tried to thank God for seeing me through the journey and bringing me to the end. Instead of words, all I could muster was a lump in my throat. I had thanked the Lord a thousand times along the way for every fall, every angel, and every prayer of a friend. But now my tears would have to thank Him for completion and the joy of going on with Him.

When I stood up, the cheering and the hugs began. I felt so honored to be surrounded by the people I loved the most.

When I asked, "Where do we go from here?" some people thought it was a great philosophical question.

Actually, I knew that Buzz had brought refreshments and I was hungry. Since it was still technically a hiking day, I didn't have to start eating normally till later!

There was so much pressure in being moved from one place to the next, that there really wasn't time that day to reflect on the meaning of finishing the hike.

After a great time of congratulations and pictures, several of us piled in a van for the twenty-mile drive out to the Big Moose Inn. Maybe after the press conference that afternoon and the celebration dinner that night I could relax. On the other hand, maybe it would be longer than I ever imagined before I could relax again.

As we drove along, someone mentioned that Orient was sitting up, looking out the back window of the van. Orient never did that. As soon as he got in a car or truck, he was down on the floor and out like a light. Did he know it was over? Did he sense that our days on the Trail had ended? Maybe he had more understanding than I did of what we were leaving behind.

Orient sat looking out the back window until we passed the gate of Baxter State Park and eased onto the paved road. Then he put his head down, closed his eyes, and crossed his paws.

For me, I had finished the A.T.

So, in the end, I guess my story is a simple one.

If you read the fifteenth chapter of Luke, it's all there in the parable of the prodigal son. It took me forty-eight years to come to my senses and say, "I will set out and go back to my father." When I did, God received me with forgiveness and opened my eyes.

Every step along the Appalachian Trail, I could see His grace and mercy. He is the only reason we made it to the end.

Chapter Twenty-One

Looking Back

I guess I had hundreds of thoughts about my trek in the last few days of the Trail, even though I really didn't have a whole lot of time to think about what it all finally meant.

The question I was asked most often was: "What does this mean to you now?"

I couldn't answer that question then. All I could see was that walking the A.T. had done something to me in terms of my faith, in terms of my physical condition, in terms of my relationships with others.

One thing thru-hikers told me at the beginning was that I'd become so adapted to the Trail's conditions that my adjustment in the other world — the real world, the world where they run thermostats, lights, switches and telephones — would be difficult. I didn't believe them then.

I do now.

Most thru-hikers look back on their Trail days as one of the most significant times in their lives. They make scrapbooks of pictures, poems, and journal entries, and tell their stories proudly to anyone willing to listen. Children and grandchildren will fall asleep to vivid descriptions of adventures on the A.T.

In every thru-hiker's memory, an investment of time, energy, and money that a lot of folks consider insane occupies a shelf labeled Commitment/Freedom. These two stand together as inseparable elements of a great enterprise

That's the way it was for me. On a two thousand-mile canvas, God had painted a stunning picture for me of the freedom that comes from the commitment to walk His way. I was still new at the business of following the Lord and hoped I'd never forget the lessons and the people of the Appalachian Trail.

I think I'm now more tolerant of people than I used to be. After the wide variety of experiences I had on the A.T., I don't think I'm as bothered by the little things as I used to be. They seem so insignificant in the overall scheme of things. Living with so many different kinds of people in such close quarters in all kinds of environments has helped me overlook and tolerate a wider variety of behavior than before.

I also came to several reconciliations and understandings along the way. Some were things I didn't know I needed to know.

I realize I could have done it another way, another trail, another route, or maybe something entirely different. It could have been anywhere, doing anything. The A.T. was only a vehicle. It was there to facilitate events that would never otherwise have happened. A lot of things were within me, internal things. It took some of the events along the way, some of the hardships, some of the solitude, to bring about new ways of thinking and believing. The Trail forced me to deal with things I'd never bothered to deal with before. That had been my way. And I have a lot more confidence now, not only in myself, but in Orient as well.

The months on the Trail also increased my faith. Or maybe it renewed my faith. During the drive back, it dawned on me how much faith I had re-gained in people. There had been times in my life when I'd become very cynical about people. But for the months I'd been on the A.T., the people experience was very, very positive, warm and reassuring. I met wonderful people the whole way.

I don't miss the pain, the loneliness, the hardships, the cold, the heat of the A.T. I never enjoyed the hiking part. It was something I felt compelled to do. It wasn't my choice.

But there are nights when I'm on the Trail again. I'm in a sleeping bag and I take a breath of that cool, invigorating air, hear Orient snuffling around in the woods, smell that forest smell, and I'm there again!

Then I awaken out of the semi-sleep state and discover I'm not out there — I was only sleeping, dreaming about the Appalachian Trail. And, in that moment, a sadness washes over me again.

Maybe I miss it more than I know.

Does Orient miss it? When we go back hiking, even for a short while, Orient is so obviously elated when he sees the Trail head that he just has a fit. He's beside himself. The first couple of hours on the Trail, he can't stand it, he wants to push, push, push. To me, he's obviously fallen in love with backpacking.

A lot of days my activity is confined to talking on the telephone all day and Orient gets bored with that. Orient has the need to get out and run, to go in the woods and — I think — to relive some of the things we did on the Trail. He'd go back on the Trail right now. Immediately. He hasn't forgotten the Appalachian Trail.

It was a growing experience for Orient. He didn't like it at first, then he eventually learned to love it. But unlike most people, he made the transition from Seeing Eye dog in the city to dog guide on the Trail and back again easily.

Would I recommend it to someone else? I don't know. The A.T. is very risky. There is an awful lot of risk in setting aside six months of your life and living a new lifestyle. But the biggest risk is the return. Since I've returned to Burlington, I've seen people I came to care about have trouble with the transition back into this world. Once you've been out there, a lot of people have difficulty returning. I have even heard of people who have committed suicide because they couldn't make that return. Others tell me they've got to keep hiking, keep trying to recover that "Trail magic." I tell them that retreating back to the Trail isn't going to solve their problems.

I just spent a weekend with the Appalachian Long Distance Hikers' Association convention in Pipe Stem, West Virginia. A lot of the people I talked to there are still looking for the same things they hoped to resolve before they started on the Trail. And when they didn't discover them, they instead decided to go to another trail, or spend six months discovering the bottom of the Grand Canyon.

I can see how other people fall into this trap, especially people who didn't find the Trail as physically difficult as I did. The Trail is a good escape from reality, and there's the whole social experience of the thru-hiker "family" and "Trail magic." But it is unrealistic to expect the wilderness to resolve a lot of issues for you, issues you've never resolved anywhere else. Sometimes it is easier to be a part of a community moving nearly two thousand miles than it is to confront and resolve deep personal problems and questions right there at home.

As a counselor, I know they're just buying time to resolve the issues they want to resolve, but don't know how.

My advice to such people is, "The answer is not on the Trail. It's in *you*. You can't get away from *you* atop Mount Katahdin. You're still there. I don't have all of the answers and I never will. But I know this: You don't need the Appalachian Trail to find yourself. You struggle with your problems in the reality of the world you left behind."

I think it is clear from this book where I found my Answer.

—Bill Irwin, Autumn 1991

Epilogue by Carolyn Starling

An Unforgettable Eight Months

I met Bill Irwin after a Sunday night service at church a couple of years ago. We talked and laughed for a long time during that first meeting, and he struck me as being like the big brother I had always wished for. Because he was blind, I felt he accepted me for who I was on the inside. It was nice to talk to someone without worrying whether my slip was showing or my mascara smeared.

When I agreed to coordinate the activities of Bill's support team at church, I thought it would involve packing some food into boxes, answering a little mail, and getting an occasional phone call if there was some kind of emergency or pressing need. When Bill called me from Neel's Gap after only four days on the Trail, I wondered if I was in over my head.

Bill needed a ski pole to replace the one he had left in his friend's truck. Could I get one and send it to him via United Parcel Service at Fontana Dam? Twenty-six pounds of clothing and equipment he didn't need were on the way back to me. Could I keep it and mail some things back as he needed them? Along with the equipment were a dozen scraps of paper with names of people scribbled on them. Could I make sure they received the newsletter that he started to tell people about his journey, or a Bible, or an answer to their questions? I hung up with my head spinning

ACROSS THE USA IN SPORTS

USA TODAY
Sports
THURSDAY, NOVEMBER 15, 1990

Step by Step: Blind hiker on h...

Courage, perseverance fuel 'The Orient Express'

FRIENDS
FIND END
OF TRAIL
BLIND HIKER NEARS
END OF COURAGEOUS
WALKING

Blind man, guide d...
tackle Appalachian...

...few hundred miles were rough wi...
...ttered feet and paws...
...ide dog.

LOTTERY

Boston Sunday Globe
SUNDAY, NOVEMBER 18, 1990

Blind faith along Appalachian Trail

The Charlotte Observer
Sunday, August 5, 1990

Blind Hiker: 'One Miracle After Another'
2,100-Mile Trail Tackled With Dog
BY JACK HORAN

The Philadelphia Inquirer
DAILY MAGAZINE
PEOPLE • HOME • MOVIES • THE ARTS • TV • STYLE
SECTION D
TUESDAY
August 21, 1990

Alone on the Appalachian Trail, Bill Irwin has endured harsh weather and brutal terrain. Yet 1,500 miles into his journey, he is confident that the Lord — and his guide dog — will lead him from the wilderness.

Epilogue by Carolyn Starling

An Unforgettable Eight Months

I met Bill Irwin after a Sunday night service at church a couple of years ago. We talked and laughed for a long time during that first meeting, and he struck me as being like the big brother I had always wished for. Because he was blind, I felt he accepted me for who I was on the inside. It was nice to talk to someone without worrying whether my slip was showing or my mascara smeared.

When I agreed to coordinate the activities of Bill's support team at church, I thought it would involve packing some food into boxes, answering a little mail, and getting an occasional phone call if there was some kind of emergency or pressing need. When Bill called me from Neel's Gap after only four days on the Trail, I wondered if I was in over my head.

Bill needed a ski pole to replace the one he had left in his friend's truck. Could I get one and send it to him via United Parcel Service at Fontana Dam? Twenty-six pounds of clothing and equipment he didn't need were on the way back to me. Could I keep it and mail some things back as he needed them? Along with the equipment were a dozen scraps of paper with names of people scribbled on them. Could I make sure they received the newsletter that he started to tell people about his journey, or a Bible, or an answer to their questions? I hung up with my head spinning and no idea where to start. By the time Bill reached Hot Springs, N.C., I had become his press secretary and was fielding eight or ten calls a week from reporters. When an article appeared in *USA Today* and was followed by a story on ABC's *World News Tonight*, the calls jumped to thirty a day.

Bill began referring almost every request for an interview to me, and I became the official information source for anyone who had a question or wanted to contact him. Often, from the time I got home from work until 11:00 p.m., I was on the phone with a pencil in one hand and a cup of coffee in the other. The *Appalachian Trail Data Book*, which listed every shelter, road crossing and mountain peak on the entire A.T., became my constant companion.

Locating Bill on the Trail was an art, not a science, and some people became impatient when I couldn't tell them exactly when and where he could be found. The best I could do was give them an approximate location and say, "If the Lord wants you to find him, you will." When one TV producer said that wasn't good enough for him, I got a little exasperated and said, "I'm sorry, my friend, but that's as good as it gets."

As the requests and phone calls began to multiply, Bill told me I could resign any time I wanted to. He said: "Look, you have a husband and two children at home, plus a full-time job. Any of those is more important than what I'm doing."

I laughed and told him that God had called me to do this, just like He had called him to hike the Trail. Bill didn't argue, but he told me to hand it off any time it got to be too much.

The worst experience for me began with an ominous phone call. One morning in June, a reporter called asking if Bill and Orient were all right. I told him they were fine as far as I knew, then asked a guarded question, "Do you have some reason to think they aren't okay?"

He hemmed and hawed a little bit, then said he'd heard a report of a Trail accident involving Bill. I thanked him for his concern and promptly called Laurie Peele at ATC headquarters in Harpers Ferry. Laurie said she couldn't speak in an official capacity, but if I wanted to ask questions, she'd answer them.

"Is Orient hurt?" I asked.

"Worse than that," Laurie replied.

"Is Bill hurt?"

"Worse," Laurie said again.

I finally asked enough questions to discover that a message had come from a reliable source saying Orient was seriously injured and Bill was dead. All I could do was hang up and wait to find out if it were true.

There was no need to call anyone else, and nothing I could do to help. I glanced at the picture of Bill and Orient on the wall of my office, and told the Lord that if Bill was already up there with Him to tell him "Hi." After that I started to cry.

People who really knew Bill joked that he would either make it all the way to Katahdin, or die trying. Being the worrier that I am, that didn't seem funny. Serious injury or death was a very real possibility for Bill every day he was on the Trail. Sighted hikers broke legs, became hypothermic, and got lost all the time. If both Bill and Orient were hurt while hiking alone, it could be a long time before anyone happened along to help. One of the most difficult things for me was leaving the Orient Express in God's hands, and letting Him be in charge of protecting them.

Six hours after that first message left me stunned, the phone rang and it was Bill Irwin. He told me that the reports of his demise were greatly exaggerated and he was fine. In fact, dying had worked out pretty well for him that day. He had arrived at a ranger station to find a search party going out to look for his body. While they tried to sort out where the rumor had started and why, Bill got a free lunch, half a gallon of ice cream, and all the cold sodas he could drink. He wondered if we could arrange reports of his death on a regular basis.

I said, "Bill Irwin, so help me, if you die again, I'm going to kill you!"

The next reports of his death, and there were several, were easier to handle.

It's safe to say that the Orient Express became the focal point of our family. There wasn't a day that we didn't think about them and pray for them. My husband, Bill Starling, is a gifted composer and singer. He wrote a beautiful song called Maker of Mountains, and sang it for the first time with a quartet at our church. The words are stamped in my mind:

> *A blind and weary traveler plods along the trail,*
> *The way is rough and rocky, at each turn fear assails.*
> *I must keep moving onward, telling others about the*
>   *One,*
> *Who saves me and keeps me, until my race is run.*
> *When your mountains are many, and you stumble and*
>   *fall,*
> *Blind eyes can see his glory, deaf ears can hear his call*
> *When the way seems dark and dreary,*
> *And your back's against the wall,*
> *Look to the Maker of mountains, and Master over all.*

All my life, I've felt less useful than others in the service of God. I can't sing, speak to groups, or give lots of money. It came as a complete surprise to discover a sense of usefulness in helping Bill. It forced me out of my comfort zone, made me pray and think creatively.

Early in the hike, I wrote several small town postmasters alerting them to the importance of the food boxes they were holding for Bill. Later, I learned that, after receiving my letter, some of them had stayed late to make sure Bill got his food when he came through. It was the first time in my life I had asked God to use me in helping someone else, and seen the answer in such an unmistakable way.

Bill Irwin is one of the finest people I know. He's kind, sensitive, caring, fun-loving, and dedicated to God in a wonderfully practical way. There's no one I respect more than him.

Bill had a trio of short answers to a lot of questions people asked along the Trail. "Pray about it." "Trust the Lord." "Talk to Carolyn."

The last one created just about the most interesting eight months I can remember.

◆◆◆

More About Orient

Most people didn't stop with just one question about Orient. They wanted to know his age, how long I'd had him, what he ate, where he slept, and how he was able to find the Trail.

I wanted to know how he managed to get so many hugs from the ladies.

Orient was born June 6, 1987, at the Seeing Eye Breeding Kennel in Mendham Township, New Jersey. He was one of two males in a litter of seven.

His mother's name was Lilac. According to Dr. Marion Jerszyk, director of the kennel, Lilac was one of the smartest German Shepherds they had ever had. A staff member at the kennel came to weigh Lilac's puppies when they were a few days old. She put the puppies in a basket, latched the door on Lilac's pen, and headed down the hall to the scale. A few moments later, the woman felt something brush her leg and looked down to find Lilac walking beside her with her nose next to the basket. Lilac had removed the clip, unlatched the door of her pen, and joined her brood.

The next day, when the puppies were taken to be examined and vaccinated, it happened again. Lilac was the only dog they ever had who could undo the latch on her pen.

Orient's father was named Mozart. He was a large, handsome dog with an extraordinary personality and a sweet disposition, traits he produced regularly in his offspring.

Each litter of Seeing Eye puppies is named from a single letter of the alphabet, according to when the litter was born during the year. So Orient's brother was Obi, and his sisters were Odessa, Olivia, Ongi, Oprah, and Ottie.

For the first two months of Orient's life, he lived at the Breeding Kennel and was regularly taken out on the spacious lawn and the puppies' play area. He took his turn on the little obstacles, and I'm sure must have impressed everyone with his skill. (The kennel is located on top of a hill in a quiet, rural setting in the beautiful Washington Valley. I guess he was a mountain dog from the beginning.)

At nine weeks, Orient went to live with a 4-H family in a nearby state and became the responsibility of a child in the family for the next year. He learned to respond to his name and received the basic elements of dog manners and obedience training from the 4-H child. In addition, he learned to be around other dogs and people in a variety of settings. Most importantly, he learned to give and receive a lot of love.

I have no idea who the family is that kept Orient, or where they live. The Seeing Eye has wisely adopted a policy of complete anonymity for the 4-H families who raise the puppies.

I think the most difficult experience of Orient's life must have been leaving the 4-H family and coming to the kennel at the Seeing Eye training facility in Morristown. The only thing I can compare it to would be my moving out of my nice, quiet house as an adult and moving into a freshman dormitory at some party college. It had to be traumatic for Orient after bonding with that family to go back to life with a bunch of dogs.

Of course, knowing him, Orient got a lot of rest before his next phase of training began. (I think he could sleep through anything, anywhere.)

His life of leisure ended when he had to start school. For twelve weeks, Orient was in a class with ten dogs and one instructor from the Seeing Eye. He learned to pull in harness and respond to the basic guiding commands: Forward, left, right, come, fetch, steady, rest, and others. He walked a lot of miles on the sidewalks of Morristown and the nearby country roads with his trainer, Doug Bohl.

When Orient was out of harness during his training, he was treated like any other pet and showered with a lot of love and petting. But when the harness was slipped over his head and shoulders, his attitude changed and he became all business. He became serious, eager to walk, and eager to guide the instructor safely around obstacles in a variety of settings.

Orient is my third dog guide. We completed our training period together at The Seeing Eye on the day before Thanksgiving, 1988. We've been fast friends from the day we met.

One of Orient's first adjustments was learning to understand a man who grew up in Alabama, lived in North Carolina, and talked like no one he had ever come across in New Jersey. Down south, "rest" is a two-syllable word. He did pretty well with it, though, and it only took him one time to know that when I said, "Do you want a cookie?" I was holding a dog biscuit behind my back.

He's also the most verbal dog I've ever been around. He has a lot of little grunts, growls, and "owwwrrs" that seem to express his opinion on just about every matter at hand. I'm still surprised at the inflection he has in his voice and the way he seems to understand exactly what I say when I talk to him.

At home in Burlington, Orient's life was very regimented. He ate twice a day when I gave him food and eliminated four times a day when I took him outside. For our first year and a half together, his feet were either on concrete or carpet because that was the context in which we lived. I knew that hiking the Appalachian Trail was going to be a bigger change for him than it was for me.

And it was. But so was coming home. Orient spent several months relearning what he forgot during our long trek in the wilderness. Since his training is my job, I take full responsibility for his mistakes, even the most embarrassing ones.

He doesn't complain about life in the city, but I know that the Appalachian Trail changed him, just as it did me. Orient came to love everything about the A.T. and the people on it. I wish I could read his mind or talk to him about what he learned.

We've gone back for a few short hikes and each time, I can sense his excitement. As soon as I take his pack out of the closet, he whines in anticipation. With the first steps on the Trail, there's a new spring in his walk.

ACKNOWLEDGMENTS

Orient and I never could have finished the Trail without the love, encouragement, and help of hundreds of people along the way. I wish there were room for every name and every deed of kindness. This is my chance to say thanks to a few:

Carolyn Starling — for conducting a symphony of volunteers from the overture through the finale, always believing that God could do the impossible.

Bill and Cortni Starling — for allowing her to keep on until the last note was played.

People's Memorial Christian Church, Burlington, North Carolina, **Rev. and Mrs. Max Allman, members of the Lightbearer's Sunday School Class, and the entire congregation** — for their prayers and gifts of love.

Support team members: Sally Bookout, Gail Reams, Carolyn Zimmerman, Charles and Dixie Stafford, Georgia Wagoner, Tim Satterfield, Truman Smythe, Marvin and Mary Lou Barts, Terri Livingston, and Wanda Grant — who packed food, mailed Bibles, published newsletters, answered mail, and handled details.

Anna Vail — for help along the Trail, a thousand errands, and the best beef jerky.

Dennis Murphy, Doug Roberts, Lea Bolling, Rosemary Carroll and all the wonderful folks at The Seeing Eye in Morristown, New Jersey — for a new vision of life. . . for independence and freedom. . . for Jorie, Sailor, and Orient.

Appalachian Trail Thru-Hikers, "Class of 1990" — for every hug, handshake, and word of encouragement along the way. Special appreciation to loyal comrades: **Gary Appleby** (The Englishman), **Art Batchelder** (AB Positive), **Sally Burgess** (Ms. Mainerd B) and **Peter Martel** (Mr. Moleskin).

Rick and Shirley Alexander (The Total Recs), **Bill Allen** (Mr. Beel), **John Carter** (John The Baptist), **Margaret Dahlgren** (Moleskin Meg), **Paul Fitzsimmons** (The Irish Goat), **Ruth Gooden** (Midnight Express), **Norenne Hogan** (Psych Hiker), **Carol Moore** (Lagunatic), **John Mesereau** (Big Mez), **Steve Miller** (Talus), **Jeff Morgan** (Bearman), **Kate O'Leary** (Smilin' Kate), **Hugh Penn** (High Pockets), **James Richmond** (Body), **Bill and Jane Robertson** (Wild Bill and Calamity Jane), **Robert Rhodes** (Sweet Old Bob), **Al and Elaine Sanborn** (Footloose and Fancy Free), **David Simmons** (The Walkin Dude), **Linda Tatsapaugh** (Hunger Hiker), **Ken Wadness** (Peace Walker), **Jeff Walker** (Skywalker), **Ray and Louise** (Special Forces), **Luke and Kristen** (The Journeyman and The Journalist) **Michael and Carolyn** (Wordman and Trail Thing)**, Ruth and Charlie** (Jersey Ruth and Red Van Charlie), **Polly and Steve** (The Moseys).

Jean Cashin, Laurie Peele, David Startzell and Brian King of the Appalachian Trail Conference — for keeping the dream alive and the Trail unbroken from Maine to Georgia.

Jeff and Dorothy Hansen — for great equipment and wise advice all the way to Maine.

Karen Padgett — for her expert repair and reconstruction of Orient's pack.

Kent and Nancy Garland, Keith and Pat Shaw, Larry and Pat Wyman, Cindy Ross and Todd Gladfelter, Father Joe Egan and Father Bosco Schmidt — for their hearts and homes.

Glen Eller of Hiawassee, Georgia — who made Hebrews 13:2 come alive.

John and Ed, day-hikers from Atlanta — whose last names and addresses dissolved in my sweaty shorts.

David Grimes — who provided most of the equipment, prayers and New York Nickels for the hike.

Walt McDougal, of **Appalachian Outfitters** — for helping select and provide equipment. **Omega Sports** — clothing, **L.L. Bean management and order department** — for wonderful care packages, **Patagonia** — rain gear, **Wolverine** — hiking boots, **Vasque** — hiking boots.

Peter Limmer and Sons — Thanks, Carl.

Sheila Beasley — for salad and prayer at Fontana Dam.

Ed and Emily Lough — for many kind gestures on and off the Trail.

Tim, Debbie, and Emily Boyer, of Duncannon, Pennsylvania — for hospitality.

The Gentrys, from Hot Springs, North Carolina — for the biggest apple I've ever eaten.

Mary Kay, Duncannon, Pennsylvania — for ice cream and other kindnesses.

All National, State, and Local Park Services and National Forest Service Agencies — for their continual assistance and encouragement from Georgia to Maine.

John and Mitzi, Apple Valley Inn — for Alabama cooking and southern hospitality.

Postmasters in Trail towns — who opened early and stayed late to deliver my food, equipment and mail.

Reuben Rajala and Peter Williams of the Appalachian Mountain Club — for their willing help; the hospitality of the **staff at Pinkham Notch Camp and Hut Crews** in the White Mountains.

Tom and Nancy Belvin, Brownville Junction, Maine — for the hospitality of their home.

Ron Theriault of Rumford, Maine — for his companionship and guidance through a tough section of the Trail.

All Appalachian Trail Club Chapters and volunteers — for maintaining the Trail.

All those who stopped — to pick up a blind hiker and his Seeing Eye dog who were hitchhiking on the road between Georgia and Maine.

Truman and Lois Smythe — for visits, care packages and prayers.

My sister, Midge, brothers Lynn and Don, my Uncle Jimmy and other family members — for their relentless prayers, support and visits.

My grandson, Jonathan — for his help with the press in Baxter State Park.

Phil Pepin — for being my untiring hiking companion and landlord for ten days in Maine.

John Morgan and the Maine Appalachian Trail Club — for providing information and support through the beautiful state of Maine.

Hill's Pet Products — for Orient's food.

Buzz and Jan Caverly, Jean Hookwater, and the staff of Baxter State Park — for service far beyond the call of duty.

Dr. Wayman Spence and his wife, Donna — for their interest, initiative, and perseverance in commemorating my journey of faith.

Bill Makepeace — who led me to personal faith in Jesus Christ, visited and encouraged me along the way.

Members of the press, newspaper, television, and radio — who faithfully reported the reason behind the hike and the One who deserves all the credit.

Alice Cary and Helen Gingras — for their many visits with goodies.

Rev. Ron and Sue Chaffee and family, and the First United Methodist Church of Brownville Junction — for allowing four weary hikers to sleep in their basement.

A note from Dave: Special thanks from Dave McCasland to **Dan Foster**, Mountain Chalet, Colorado Springs, for excellent advice and equipment.

The photographers who so kindly walked, shared sleeping quarters, and so on with me, and whose work is shown in this book — and especially Bill Greene, USA 1988 Photographer of the Year.

Finally, and perhaps most importantly, to Dave McCasland, with whom I began a business relationship in the White Mountains of New Hampshire, and who became a forever friend and my spiritual mentor.

People Making A Difference

Family Bookshelf offers the finest in good wholesome Christian literature, written by best-selling authors. All books are recommended by an Advisory Board of distinguished writers and editors.

We are also a vital part of a compassionate outreach called **Bowery Mission Ministries**. Our evangelical mission is devoted to helping the destitute of the inner city.

Our ministries date back more than a century and began by aiding homeless men lost in alcoholism. Now we also offer hope and Gospel strength to homeless, inner-city women and children. Our goal, in fact, is to end homelessness by teaching these deprived people how to be independent with the Lord by their side.

Downtrodden, homeless men are fed and clothed and may enter a discipleship program of one-on-one professional counseling, nutrition therapy and Bible study. This same Christian care is provided at our women and children's shelter.

We also welcome nearly 1,000 underprivileged children each summer at our Mont Lawn Camp located in Pennsylvania's beautiful Poconos. Here, impoverished youngsters enjoy the serenity of nature and an opportunity to receive the teachings of Jesus Christ. We also provide year-round assistance through teen activities, tutoring in reading and writing, Bible study, family counseling, college scholarships and vocational training.

During the spring, fall and winter months, our children's camp becomes a lovely retreat for religious gatherings of up to 200. Excellent accommodations include heated cabins, chapel, country-style meals and recreational facilities. Write to Paradise Lake Retreat Center, Box 252, Bushkill, PA 18324 or call: (717) 588-6067.

Bowery Mission Ministries are supported by voluntary contributions of individuals and bequests. Contributions are tax deductible. Checks should be made payable to Bowery Mission.

 **Fully accredited Member of the Evangelical Council for Financial Accountability**

Every Monday morning, our ministries staff joins together in prayer. If you have a prayer request for yourself or a loved one, simply write to us.

 Administrative Office: 40 Overlook Drive, Chappaqua, New York 10514 Telephone: (914) 769-9000